WELL WITH MY SOUL

Four Dramatic Stories of Great Hymn Writers

Rachael Phillips

BARBOUR
PUBLISHING

For a complete list of Heroes of the Faith titles, see page 208.

© 2003 by Barbour Publishing, Inc.

ISBN 1-58660-916-5

All Scripture quotations are taken from the King James Version of the Bible.

Cover illustration © Dick Bobnick.

Published by Barbour Publishing, Inc., P.O. Box 719, Uhrichsville, Ohio 44683, www.barbourbooks.com

Our mission is to publish and distribute inspirational products offering exceptional value and biblical encouragement to the masses.

ecpa Member of the
Evangelical Christian
Publishers Association

Printed in the United States of America.
5 4 3 2 1

WELL WITH MY SOUL

CONTENTS

introduction

When peace, like a river, attendeth my way,
When sorrows like sea-billows roll,
Whatever my lot, Thou has taught me to say,
"It is well, it is well with my soul."

Horatio Gates Spafford, a lawyer, wrote these now-familiar words as he watched the icy waves of the Atlantic roll over the spot where his four little girls, Annie, Maggie, Bessie, and baby Tanetta, had drowned in a shipwreck days before. In an effort to forget his business problems back in Chicago, Horatio had planned to join his family on a European vacation. But only his grieving wife, Anna, the lone survivor, now awaited him in France.

While some find this portion of Horatio Spafford's life familiar, few know how he gave of himself before this tragedy during the Great Fire of Chicago in 1871, or afterward in Jerusalem. Fewer still know the stories of Philip Bliss, William Cowper, and Frances Havergal. Bliss, an uneducated farm boy, rose to international prominence as a composer associated with Dwight L. Moody. He wrote gospel hymns like "Hallelujah, What a Savior" and "My Redeemer," and composed the music to

Spafford's "It Is Well with My Soul" not long before his own untimely death. A century before Spafford and Bliss, the famous English poet William Cowper struggled with suicidal depression. His songs, such as "God Moves in a Mysterious Way" and "There Is a Fount," lit a candle of faith in his own darkness and dispelled the doubts of many who have since sung his hymns. Frances Havergal, a brilliant clergyman's daughter, wrote hymns such as "Take My Life and Let It Be" and "Like a River Glorious." Willingly she devoted her immense musical and intellectual gifts—and some of the family treasure—to Jesus Christ.

Like their Old Testament forerunner King David, all four hymn writers sang of pain and joy, mourning and celebration, doubt and confidence in God. As the Master Musician wove together the major and minor melodies of their lives, it was well with their souls.

HORATIO
SPAFFORD

one

W hat a magnificent night!" Elizabeth Harris exclaimed. The moonlight gleamed in her hair, light-
ing her face as if the moon thought someone should
paint her portrait. She and other teenagers drank lemonade on
an elegant veranda in Troy, New York, celebrating the end of
school, 1846.

Horatio Gates Spafford, whose father owned the house,
tried not to stare at the girl. His friend Charlie had brought her
to his family's party, and he did not want to appear rude. Horatio
felt more at ease discussing classics and poetry than making
small talk. He said little as the group chatted and joked, savor-
ing their free time after examinations were done.

"There's the North Star! And the Dippers are so clear
tonight!" marveled Charlie.

The others echoed Charlie's and Elizabeth's rapture at the
beauty of the night sky, until Horatio could stand it no longer.

"The galaxies are indeed wonderful—"

"You should know, Horatio," said Charlie. "You're always
writing poems about the stars."

"Their beauty is overcast, indistinct, cloudy. Yet everyone
talks endlessly of their outstanding brilliance. Now, Charlie,
be candid. Be honest. Do you really see enough beauty up

there to warrant your outburst?"[1]

The others stared at Horatio. Charlie's jaw dropped. His friend was usually pleasant, always rational. Had Horatio studied too hard this past term?

Then an idea struck Charlie. "Here," he said, handing his glasses to Horatio. "Try these."

Horatio glared at Charlie as if he were insane, but he put the spectacles on. A gasp escaped him, then another.

"Horatio, you're nearsighted," said Charlie.

Horatio did not answer. He stood transfixed by the hundreds of diamonds that sparkled above him in clean, crystalline beauty.

His discovery inspired him to write a poem—"Night":

Ye countless stars that tremble in the sky,
How bright and beautiful are you tonight!
I've known ye long, but never did my eye
So burn beneath the glory of your light
As it doth now; I kneel to ye—ye wear
The impress of the Deity that's there.[2]

Once his physical vision was corrected, Horatio wasted no time in scrutinizing his intellectual vision. He no longer swallowed traditional viewpoints, those of others or himself, without inquiry. He examined issues, loosening and peeling away layers of conventionality with sharp questions. *How do we know this? Why?*

Every clear night he sat on his porch steps and marveled at the magnificent unexplored universe he had underestimated for years. *All my life I had no inkling of the beauty or complexity of Your creation, God. What else have I overlooked because I never questioned my own limited view?*

Horatio was born on October 20, 1828, the son of an eminent historian and horticulturist. His hometown recognized his early promise as he won scholastic and literary prizes. After his starstruck epiphany, Horatio completed law school, and in 1856 a passion for adventure drove him to the endless Midwestern prairies, to the raw, up-and-coming city of Chicago on the shores of Lake Michigan. Horatio threw himself into law and politics. A fervent opponent of slavery before the Civil War and later a supporter of Abraham Lincoln, he soon made his views known in Chicago-area rallies. As Horatio's wealth and influence grew, he made generous contributions to many community projects. Science fascinated him. As professor of medical jurisprudence, Horatio became one of the first faculty members of the budding Lind University, whose medical department eventually developed into the Northwestern University's Feinberg School of Medicine.

The dynamic young bachelor did not go unnoticed in social circles. No longer a shy teenager, Horatio became a sought-after dinner guest in many prominent households. He found himself the target of Chicago's marriage-minded mamas.

"Dear Mr. Spafford," said a cultured, feminine voice at Horatio's elbow. He turned from his fascinating after-church theological conversation with his pastor and gave a mental sigh. Mrs. Smythe-Merrifield, a formidable society matron in yards of steel-colored silk and an oversized feathered hat, smiled at him with predatory eagerness. Her pale daughter Paulina trailed behind her. Horatio bowed and smiled and hoped for an early escape.

"I understand you live in Clifton House downtown," said the lady, blocking his path with practiced ease.

"Yes, madam, it is close to my work."

"So convenient for you! Yet I know their dining is not the best. Do join us today for a home-cooked meal, Mr. Spafford."

Horatio looked at Mrs. Smythe-Merrifield's tiered pearl necklace and silver lace gloves. He doubted if she had so much as poured herself a glass of water in years. "I—"

"Do not deny us this opportunity to share our blessings," said Mrs. Smythe-Merrifield, tugging Paulina forward.

"I'm sorry, madam," said Horatio, "but I have accepted another invitation." He did not tell her that three other mothers in the congregation already had extended "Christian charity" to him, the lonely, rich young bachelor! Horatio escaped their clutches and focused his energies on building his career and serving his community. He became active in the city's religious affairs, teaching Sunday school in his Presbyterian church, where he met the love of his life, Anna Larssen, a gifted immigrant Norwegian girl. He married her in 1861, much to the dismay of Mrs. Smythe-Merrifield and other aristocratic matriarchs. Over the next decade, the Spaffords became the parents of four beautiful baby girls.

Horatio had achieved every man's dream: a highly successful career, a loving family, the respect and admiration of his community. But though a devout Christian, he felt unsatisfied. *Why?* he asked himself. *What do I lack?* he asked God.

One day during his lunch break, he heard Dwight L. Moody preach from the courthouse steps at the corner of Randolph and Clark Streets in Chicago.

"What is repentance?"

The stocky speaker dressed in the long frock coat would not ordinarily impress Horatio, whose influence now penetrated the courts, colleges, newspapers, businesses, and banks of post-Civil War Chicago. He himself was a far more imposing figure: tall and dark-haired, with a swordlike mind that affixed wrongdoers and wavering judges to justice as if it were a wall.

But Horatio could not take his eyes off Moody.

"You see, repentance is deeper than feeling," said the evangelist. "It is action. It is turning right about. And God commands all men everywhere to turn."[3]

Moody continued to preach in the noonday sunshine. Drivers of passing wagons slowed to gawk. Workmen with tin lunch buckets paused in munching their cold biscuits and salt pork. Harried businessmen halted in surprise. Soon a crowd of a hundred circled the courthouse steps, with more wandering over to hear the evangelist. *They say he sells shoes during the week,* thought Horatio, *and I bet he's an excellent salesman. But this is far more than good salesmanship. What a storyteller! Makes me think of Jesus' parables. . . .*

Before Moody's hearers realized it, they were clutching

14

imaginary luggage and riding a hypothetical train to Chicago with him. Horatio felt a stab of dismay when the evangelist's make-believe friend informed him he was on the wrong train:

Mr. Doan comes down and he says, "Mr. Moody, where are you going?"

And I say, "Going to Chicago. . ."

"Well, sir, I tell you, you are wrong. That train is not going to Chicago at all; it is going to take you right in an opposite direction. That train is going off to New York, and if you want to go to Chicago, you must get out of that train and get aboard another."

I did not believe him at first.

"Well," he says, "but I have been here in this city for twenty-five years. I know all about these trains. . . . I tell you that I am right, and you are wrong, sir. You are on the wrong train."

At last Mr. Doan convinces me that I am on the wrong train. That is conviction. But, if I do not change trains, I will go to New York in spite of my conviction. That is not repentance. I will tell you what is repentance. Grabbing my bag and running and getting on the other train. That is repentance.

Now, you are on the wrong train, my friends, and what you want is to change trains tonight. You are on the wrong side of this question. You are for the god of this world, and the world claims your influence. God commands all men now everywhere to repent. Change trains! Make haste! There is no time for delay![4]

All day Horatio pondered Moody's words. He listened to the evangelist the next day, then the next.

Every night I have repented of my sins since I was a child, Lord. But this man makes me want to forget the greed of pursuing wealth and power, the tiresomeness of bland, comfortable Christianity. There's more to the life You've given me. Show me, Lord. Show me.

Just as Horatio's discovery of the stars as a schoolboy had revolutionized his perspective of the constellations, the preaching of Dwight L. Moody had changed the wealthy lawyer's life forever.

As usual, Horatio translated his beliefs into immediate action. He helped Moody organize noontime devotional meetings of prayer and worship for business and professional men. Soon thousands of men spent their lunch hours together on their knees, praying for God's power to change their town.

Horatio conducted jail meetings, visited hospitals, and devoted his considerable fortune to evangelistic and benevolent causes. Never afraid to speak his mind, Horatio inspired respect in even his most cynical associates because of his concern for the lost and needy of Chicago.

He became one of Moody's financial supporters. In 1870 he and several other businessmen, including the owner of the shoe store where Moody had worked, signed an agreement to pay the evangelist a salary so he could preach full-time. Horatio sometimes disagreed with Moody, as he felt the evangelist placed too much emphasis on God's judgment and not enough on His love. As usual, he made his position clear to his friend and spiritual mentor. But Horatio believed God had used Moody to change his own life and viewed him as the means to help others change, too.

His close association with Moody later generated warm friendships with musicians Ira Sankey, Philip Bliss, and George Stebbins, as well as Major Daniel Webster Whittle, an evangelist in his own right. Many nights the Spafford home rang with the prayers, songs, and laughter of these architects of the American revivalist movement.

Horatio Gates Spafford had discovered a new spiritual frontier, and he wanted to soar high in the heavens, among the stars.

two

I wish I did not have to go to Indiana," Horatio told his wife.

"Do you have to leave, Papa?" asked seven-year-old Maggie. Named after Horatio's favorite sister, his second daughter seemed more sensitive than her siblings. Already a tear trickled down her chubby cheek.

"Only for a couple of days, Maggie Lee!" said her father, picking her up and waltzing across the parlor. She giggled, forgetting her fears.

Anna's blue eyes embraced her husband. Although they had been married more than ten years, Horatio melted. That direct gaze had fascinated him from the moment fifteen-year-old Anna entered the Sunday school class he taught. Although pleasant and respectful, she had demanded answers to her unapologetic questions about Christianity. As a child, she had lost her mother and baby brother in a cholera epidemic. She had also nursed her tubercular father until his death, working hard and living on a farm in northern Minnesota, where Indian raids threatened their safety. Where was God when she and her family were suffering? During the following weeks, Horatio explained his position to Anna, challenged her reasoning, and guided her to faith in Christ. A year later he asked the musically gifted, striking Norwegian blond girl to marry him but found, to his chagrin, that she was

17

only sixteen—fourteen years younger than himself! Her maturity had fooled Horatio. He agreed with her older sister, with whom she lived, that Anna was too young for marriage. For three long years, Anna attended the Ferry Institute for Young Ladies in Lake Forest, twenty-eight miles from Chicago. The wait only intensified their feelings; Horatio haunted the school like a lovesick ghost, and soon Anna scratched their initials in her dormitory window with her engagement ring. On September 5, 1861, the two finally married. Anna had worn a pretty but practical navy blue dress, her flaxen hair crowned with a navy bonnet trimmed with pink rosebuds. Because of the Civil War, the two had planned a simple ceremony with few witnesses.

But our friends sneaked into the church and filled it with white flowers. They all came to share the happiest day of our lives! remembered Horatio. He still could see the altar, nearly covered with fragrant blossoms as they said their marriage vows. *They were beautiful. But not as lovely as Anna that day. Or now.*

"Return as soon as you can," said Anna to her husband. Although a strong, capable woman, she disliked his absences almost as much as Maggie.

"I will," promised Horatio, "but it's important we sell this property along Lake Michigan to a businessman of this caliber—important to Chicago's development and important to our finances." He and several partners had purchased extensive holdings along the lake. Horatio saw the success of this investment as key to downgrading his law practice so he could spend more time doing what he loved—promoting the gospel of Jesus Christ.

Anna nodded as Annie, nine, and Bessie, five, clattered downstairs to say good-bye.

"You're so noisy, Bessie! You'll wake Tanetta!" scolded Annie, the big sister.

"No, *you'll* wake her!"

"I do not believe Tanetta could sleep in a peaceful house," said Anna with a rueful smile. "She is so accustomed to noise!"

"A joyful noise," said Horatio, hugging his girls. He kissed Anna and waved from the buggy as Peter, his coachman and handyman, encouraged old Billy, the horse, to hasten his gait.

"We'll just make the Dummy, sir," he said to Horatio, "as long as Billy don't stop much." The Dummy was a commuter train which Horatio rode every day to downtown Chicago. It ran only twice daily, so the Spaffords' frequent dinner guests often became overnight guests.

Many visitors spent days, weeks, even months at the Spafford home, as Horatio and Anna opened their house to anyone who needed lodging or a retreat. Horatio glanced back at Anna once more before the buggy drove out of sight. Right now their guest rooms remained empty. He would do his best to avoid bringing company home. How they would enjoy spending a quiet family week or two together when he returned!

Horatio glanced around his domain as the carriage ambled down the driveway to the road. He loved Lake View, especially in October when his twelve acres erupted with fall colors. Maples waved their brilliant red and gold leaves like banners over their quaint gabled cottage covered with ivy. Lake Michigan sparkled in the crisp autumn air. He, Anna, and the girls often took walks in the woods, picking up acorns and watching busy squirrels. But this fall morning felt like a day in July. Horatio wiped his moist face with his spotless white handkerchief.

He frowned as the buggy continued toward the train station. The trees' foliage appeared less colorful than usual. The hot, dry wind that had roasted the prairies for weeks rattled their shriveled leaves. No one could remember a summer as hot as that of 1871. *I sure wish it would rain,* thought Horatio. Several major fires had leveled large forest areas near Chicago; small blazes ignited in the city, simply because the entire area was so parched. For the first time, a point of fear dug into his mind. *Should I leave my family right now?*

"Going to make it on time, sir!" said Peter. His honest, leathery face reassured his employer. Peter had worked for him since before Horatio's marriage and lived in a small cottage near the Spaffords. Horatio knew Peter would protect Anna and the girls before he thought of himself.

19

"All aboard!" The conductor gave a courteous nod to Horatio and took his valise.

I'll finish this business and return day after tomorrow at the latest! We'll celebrate together! No more worries about the futures of Anna and the girls. Horatio and the other commuters opened their newspapers and mopped their damp foreheads as the Dummy chugged toward Chicago.

"Mama, what's that?" Annie pointed to an odd glow in the southern horizon.

"You know it's just the city lights, Annie." Her mother had taken the girls for a swim in Lake Michigan after dinner, hoping the excursion would help the children sleep well that night. Baby Tanetta had already drifted off, and little Bessie's eyelids drooped. Anna did not bother to look at the sky, as she was intent on herding her brood home before they fell asleep on the beach!

"No, Mama," insisted the oldest girl, "the light's much bigger than usual. Is that smoke?"

Anna cuddled the baby against her shoulder and followed her daughter's gaze. Not only were large black clouds of smoke rising from the Chicago area, but Anna could also see a huge column of flame that rose before her eyes like the Biblical pillar of fire. Lake Michigan mirrored the terrifying sight.

Chicago's burning! Chicago's burning! Anna clutched her baby. If only Horatio were here! What would she do if the winds blew the fire north to their home?

"Will it burn us up?" asked Maggie, beginning to tremble.

Anna gathered her wits and the children's belongings. "Of course not," she said in a firm voice. "We live far away from the city. But we must pray for those poor people before we go to bed. Come, girls."

Later Anna gathered Peter and the three house servants together. "I don't think the fire will affect us," she said, "but the winds might blow it toward the dry forest between us and the city. We must make evacuation plans should that happen."

As she and Peter carried on a discussion about the Spafford

valuables, animals, food supplies, and transportation, Anna bade her pounding heart to calm itself. She had no idea if the trains could run or whether the fire would block northward routes from the city. But she knew Horatio would find his way back to Lake View the moment he knew of the danger—if he were able.

"Chicago in Ashes!"[1]

The headlines screamed at Horatio and drove his business deal from his mind. He dropped the toast he was buttering and skimmed the accompanying story in horror. Horatio threw his newspaper down on the restaurant table and made a frantic dash for the train station.

"I must get to Chicago!" he shouted to the agent.

"But, sir, they say the fire's out of control. The early train's running, but I have no idea if it will reach the city."

"I don't care. Sell me a ticket, man." Horatio almost leaped aboard the train, riding it along with other worried men whose families and businesses were in Chicago.

God, grant that my lovely ones are safe. Anna. Oh, Anna. My girls.

He blessed God that the train made it to the south side of the city. He left his valise aboard and headed downtown. Chaos met his eyes. Fire fringed almost every house he saw, flames licking hungrily at neighboring buildings. Wagons, carriages, buggies, and handcarts loaded with desperate people and household goods clogged the streets, lurching into each other's paths, running down pedestrians. Hundreds of men, women, and children mobbed the neighborhoods in a frantic search for escape routes and lost relatives, often trampling each other to death. Children wandered alone, screaming, their tears unheeded. Mothers with broods of little ones hunted for others they would never find. Helpless invalids lay on pallets in the street, begging for help to escape the fire.

What can I do, God? There are so many in need, so many, thought Horatio. He moved several elderly ladies to safer ground and tried to comfort a weeping mother who could not find her little boy. *But I must get to Anna and the girls. I must make sure they are safe. . . .*

Wealthy homeowners hauled elegant furniture and clothing, priceless paintings and ornate silver services from their burning mansions, offering wagon drivers fantastic amounts of money to carry them and their treasures to safety. Some guarded pianos, only to watch them explode into flames when the wooden sidewalks ignited. Looters scurried through the streets, loaded with all they could carry.

"This is it! Opportunity! Opportunity for the worker, the everyday man!" A tall, wild-looking man tossed a burning torch into a pile of mahogany furniture a fat bald man had dragged from his opulent mansion. The "prophet" continued to preach with abandon from a wooden box.

If I weren't in such a hurry, I'd knock him flat, thought Horatio.

His own office and extensive library no doubt would be plundered. *But I must make it to a bridge. I'll have to cross a bridge to make it to Lake View.* He veered toward the Chicago River and directed several bewildered women and their families to the river, too.

"Run to a bridge!" he urged. "Hurry, before they all burn and you're trapped in the city!" Horatio led an active life, walking, swimming, and cycling; he could swim the river if he had to. *But these mothers and little children. . .* "There's one still intact!" he shouted in relief. "Cross that bridge!"

"But it's burning!" said a terrified woman in a tattered evening dress. She was holding a pink-cheeked toddler in her arms.

"Only a little. Hurry, take your child before there is no way across!"

Hundreds of people already jammed the bridge; Horatio did what he could to protect the young woman as they struggled through the stampede. He breathed a sigh of relief as he finally made it to the north shore. More desperate scenes awaited him as he walked the streets—hundreds, thousands more blazing buildings, frightened mobs, hordes of vehicles smashing into each other, their drivers cursing in every language Chicago knew. Drunken men flourished bottles of beer they had stolen from empty saloons. The fevered air split with the thunder of an explosion, then another. Horatio grabbed an iron lamppost as the ground beneath him shook and cried out as the hot metal scorched his hands.

Mr. Moody often preaches of hell, Lord. Could it be worse than this? Horatio wiped his weary, sweaty face with burnt, sooty fingers.

But in the midst of his own despair, Horatio also saw heroes entering burning buildings in efforts to save strangers, some to die in the inferno themselves. He also interrupted his own desperate journey several times to rescue children and elderly screaming from upstairs windows while flames and smoke billowed from the floors below. Men and women threw their arms around the weeping and distraught, sharing food, water, blankets, and wagons. Families cared for lost children, not knowing if their parents would ever be found.

When night came, the city did not darken, still illuminated with the ghastly, unnatural glare of the fire. Neither did the winds subside. Horatio coughed as clouds of acrid, choking smoke tried to smother him. He had hoped to outrun the fire. He realized, with horror, the fire had outdistanced him with ease and was racing northward—northward toward the forest, toward Lake View. An evil dragon that engorged itself on everything living and dead in its path, the fire grew every moment.

Anna. Annie. Maggie. Bessie. Tanetta. Horatio reached the empty train station where he usually took the Dummy home. *No one here. I must go on.* Winded and weary, Horatio was forced to slow his pace to a fast walk. His own breath tasted like the filthy gray mists that swirled and eddied around him. He followed the train track north. *Help me, O God. Please keep them safe. Anna. Annie. Maggie. Bessie. Tanetta.* The names became a refrain that kept him moving, a rhythm that pushed his legs far beyond their usual strength. *Anna. Annie. Maggie. Bessie. Tanetta. . .*

"Horatio! Thank God!" Anna's sad face lit up like Fourth of July fireworks. He held her as if he would never let go.

"Papa! Papa's home!" His daughters clung to his knees, his

23

feet, his dirty, tattered coat that reeked of smoke. He kissed them all again and again. Then everyone began to talk at once.

"Girls, girls! Your father is exhausted. Let him rest and eat, then you can talk with him." Anna took Horatio's arm and led him to an armchair. "Maggie, tell Cook we need soup for Papa. Annie, bring my salve and box of bandages." She scanned his black face. "Are you hurt, Horatio?"

"Hands singed a little. Nothing like some poor souls." He shuddered.

"Anna? What is all that noise? I can't rest with such a commotion!" a querulous voice complained from a nearby room.

"My husband has returned, safe and sound, Aunty Sims, from the fire. I will send the girls outside to play a little later."

A loud "humph!" resounded, and the bedroom door shut with a bang.

"Who was that?" Horatio raised his eyebrows.

"The girls call her Aunty Sims. A wagon driver brought her when the fire began, and she has been here ever since." Anna sighed. "Her husband left her a long time ago, and no one seems in a hurry to claim her. But the children love her; she tells them wonderful stories! And she has mended every sock in the house. But she becomes cranky when her nap is interrupted." Anna brightened. "At least the fire did not reach our house."

"It stopped at Fullerton Avenue," said Horatio. "Only a few blocks from here!"

Anna nodded. "When I realized it was headed this way, I took the girls, Aunty Sims, and the Millers—"

"Who?"

"Mary Miller, my old schoolmate. She and her husband, their little ones, and her mother all showed up in their elegant carriage not long after Aunty Sims came. They were so coated with soot I thought they were colored. Mary's mother had six of her best dresses on, and the rest wore nightclothes. I couldn't imagine who these strangers were!" Her eyes twinkled a little. "We fed them and helped them to bed. But the fire drew too near, and we had to leave Lake View. We drove up Graceland

Road and lodged the night before last with a family in Jefferson, along with twenty other people. How kind they were, even though we were barely acquainted! And most of their guests were strangers to them." Anna shook her head. "We returned yesterday morning when we heard the fire had finally burned itself out. The Millers left almost immediately for the city."

"But it could still be very dangerous!" exclaimed Horatio.

"I know. The explosions continue. We feel the shaking even this far away! But Mary's father is still in Chicago," said Anna. She held her husband's face in her hands. "If I had not the girls to think of, I would have searched for you from one end of Chicago to the other."

"I know." The weariness of two days with little rest, food, or water closed in on Horatio, and he slumped into the chair.

"Don't talk now." His wife held a cup of cold water to his lips, then spooned broth into his mouth. Bessie and Maggie untied his shoes and put his slippers on the wrong feet—but Horatio did not mind.

After living through the hellish Great Fire of Chicago, coming home was heaven.

three

Two days later, to Anna's dismay, Horatio and Peter drove into Chicago. "I must see if my office survived," said Horatio. "And I'm sure the people in the city are in desperate need of help."

As he expected, the fire had devastated his beautiful office. Hundreds of legal books he had collected throughout the years lay in ashes. The fire had destroyed the entire business district. Banks, businesses, professional offices, hotels, theaters, churches, the *Chicago Tribune* building—all charred beyond recognition. Horatio felt as if he were living in a nightmare. But he removed his coat and began digging through the rubble to salvage what he could. After a few hours, he realized only a fireproof safe and its contents had survived.

Horatio and his partners, like everyone else, would have to rebuild. But the real financial devastation lay in their investment in the property along Lake Michigan. No one would be interested in expanding their holdings in downtown Chicago for quite some time! Mere survival, plus rebuilding, would absorb the resources and energy of all. Horatio had poured all his savings into the project and borrowed substantial sums to purchase the land in what had appeared the perfect investment strategy. He still had to make his interest payments, fire or no fire, especially as the banks were now strained to the utmost.

Horatio and Anna managed to retain their home, but they had to take out a mortgage. Neither cared. They had each other and their children, and they praised God for His protection and provision.

Their hearts broke, however, as they saw the suffering of their fellow Chicagoans throughout the bitter winter following the Great Fire of 1871. Lists of missing or found persons were printed every day by the *Chicago Tribune* as families sought each other. Homeless people by the hundreds struggled to survive. Hungry men, women, and children lined up to receive food and clothing sent by compassionate people throughout the world. Horatio and Anna threw all their energy and talents into the efforts of the Relief and Aid Committees. Despite his own financial difficulties, Horatio initiated the rebuilding of the YMCA, an organization he had supported before the Great Fire.

Chicago began a slow recovery.

But as Chicago made progress, Anna Spafford's health deteriorated. The Great Fire had occurred only a few months after Tanetta's birth. Horatio worried about his wife; the fire had taken an immense emotional toll on Anna. She had cared for her family, cared for refugees, cared for the homeless and hurting— cared for everyone but herself. Aunty Sims had developed a fanatical loyalty toward her kind rescuer. She had vowed never to leave Anna, and Anna could not bring herself to make her go, though Aunty Sims had recovered. So she stayed on and on, haranguing the family daily about the injustices she had suffered at her husband's hands.

"If God forgives my husband and takes him to heaven when he dies," she told the Spaffords, "I never want to set foot in the place!"

"Aunty Sims, of course you want to go to heaven," soothed Anna. "We must all learn to forgive, you know."

"Oh, it's all very well for you to talk!" scoffed Aunty Sims. "You have a splendid husband, lovely, healthy children, a beautiful home; it is easy to be grateful and good when you have everything you want. But look out that you are not a fair-weather friend to God!"[1]

Aunty Sims pushed Anna past her limits.

"You must remove your wife from this situation," said Dr. Hedges, the Spaffords' devoted family physician, to Horatio.

"I know, Doctor! But Anna will not leave the children, especially since the fire."

"Then all of you go on an extended vacation together! Anna needs relief from that Sims woman, and you must see to it."

With pleasure, thought Horatio. He had visited Europe on a business trip three years before and had always wanted to explore the continent with Anna. The Spaffords had many friends living in France and could arrange for extended child care and schooling for the children while Horatio and Anna traveled from one exciting country to another. Such an undertaking, Horatio knew, would strain the utmost limits of their finances, but nothing on earth meant more to him than his wife.

He bought tickets for his family on the grand SS *Ville du Havre*, a French liner considered the most magnificent ship in existence. Anna protested the cost. But shortly before they were to leave, a businessman offered to buy Horatio's land along Lake Michigan!

"We must not postpone our trip, Anna," said Horatio. *Any delay might make Anna's sister change her mind about keeping Aunty Sims!* he thought. "I will remain behind and meet with this man," said Horatio aloud.

"But I don't want to leave without you!" pleaded Anna.

"It will only be a short time," answered Horatio, though he could hardly bear the thought himself. "When I have closed this deal, I will immediately follow you. We will celebrate together and enjoy our vacation all the more because we leave behind almost no debt and have bright prospects when we return."

"It is a great opportunity," agreed Anna. Her reluctance diminished considerably when her close friend and neighbor, Mrs. Goodwin, decided to make the journey with her, along with her three children, Goertner, Julia, and Lulu. Other friends asked Anna to oversee their son, Willie, who was sailing on the same ship to visit his grandparents in Germany. The arrangement eased Anna's tensions and reassured Maggie, who did not want to leave Lake View and begged to stay with her father. Several French pastors who had attended Moody conferences also agreed to travel home with the group on the *Ville du Havre*.

Horatio rejoiced as his wife began to anticipate a pleasant journey with good friends. He rode the train with the group from Chicago to New York City and accompanied them to the docks, where the *Ville du Havre* sat in the water like a queen on her throne.

Change the rooms. I must change the room reservations for Anna and the girls. This impression grew in Horatio as he stood on the docks with his family. *What is the matter with me? I made those room choices myself several weeks ago. They are the best, the safest.* But the compulsion grew: *Change the rooms. Change them for rooms in the bow.*

His children shouted and laughed as the weak November sunlight sparkled in the water. Although Anna grasped Horatio's hand as if she did not want to let go, she chatted with Mrs. Goodwin as they waited.

"I must see the purser," said Horatio, "before you leave."

"But why, dear? Don't you have the tickets?"

"Of course. I simply want to check them." Horatio did not want to share his irrational fears with his wife. Nor did he intend to inform her he had received a telegram back at the hotel right before they left, notifying him his prospective buyer had died of sudden heart failure. *I will not allow any rain on Anna's sunshine,* he thought to himself. *I must take care of this by myself.*

Although a little irritable, the purser made the change in accommodations, and Horatio felt an instant sense of relief. He dashed back as the gangplank was lowered and hugged his family. Anna clung to him for a moment but turned a resolute face toward the ship. "Come, girls," she said in her best no-nonsense voice. "We will see Papa soon in France. It's time to go."

Anna. Annie. Maggie. Bessie. Tanetta. Horatio waved to all of them as the huge boat slowly made its way into the open harbor. Tanetta, who was now almost two years old, threw kisses from dimpled little hands. Horatio threw a hundred back.

Oh, God, please guard my girls until I see them again. He watched until they were out of sight.

Horatio attended a wedding on November 25, 1873, and wrote Anna a detailed description of the happy celebration with their friends and family. Many had asked about Anna and the girls, and he had told them he expected any time to receive a cable from France notifying him of their landing. Horatio took care to keep his tone positive, yet his longing seeped through the lines of his letter:

> *Day after tomorrow will be Thanksgiving Day. I will not say how I shall miss you and the dear children. But I will not think too much about that. Let us instead strive to profit by the separation. I think this separation has touched me more deeply than anything else which has ever occurred in my life. . . .*
>
> *But, never mind, my heart. If the Lord keeps us, we hope before many months to be all together again, better understanding than ever before the greatness of His mercy in the many years of the past.*
>
> *When you write, tell me all about the children. How thankful I am to God for them! May He make us faithful parents, having an eye single to His glory. Annie and Maggie and Bessie and Tanetta—it is a sweet consolation even to write their names. May the dear Lord keep and sustain and strengthen you.*[2]

Horatio had no inkling all four of his little girls had perished in the incomprehensible wreck of the *Ville du Havre* four nights before.

No news is good news. The phrase had begun to reverberate

through Horatio's head. Not a natural worrier, he could usually quiet his doubts with this phrase.

Not now.

Silence from the other side of the ocean. *No news is good news.*

Then, at last, the cable message arrived from Wales, dated December 1, 1873.

"Wales?" questioned Horatio. "Why aren't Anna and the girls in France?" A cold hand squeezed his heart. He tore it open and read the two-word message from Anna: "Saved Alone."[3]

He dropped as if shot. *Alone, Anna?*

All that night Horatio paced, his dear friend Major Whittle and others at his side. He said nothing, only walked across the room where his little ones had read stories aloud and played "princess," wearing paper crowns. He walked and walked and walked. As the night's blackness turned to the soft gray of dawn, Horatio spoke.

"I am glad to trust the Lord when it will cost me something."[4]

He cabled Anna that she should continue on to Paris with Rev. Lorriaux, a French pastor who had survived the shipwreck. Horatio knew Anna's dear friend Bertha Johnson, among others, lived in Paris and would care for her. He himself would leave for Europe as soon as he could.

The following Sunday Horatio attended church, as always.

But now he sat alone in the family pew.

He felt the compassionate eyes of friends whose hearts ached for his loss. Through his own tears he saw the tears of many who grieved with him.

But Horatio also felt the cold scrutiny of others who dissected his sorrows as if they were specimens to be explained. All Chicago knew the Spaffords had suffered devastating losses in the Great Fire of 1871. The rich, aristocratic young family had been reduced to shabby necessity. Their extravagant plans to visit Europe had been weighed and found wanting. Now, less than two years after the Great Fire, Horatio and Anna had lost all their children. Was this not evidence God was punishing some terrible sin in their lives? Were they not reaping what they had sown?

Horatio had always held his own opinions without apology. The great inventor and philanthropist Cyrus McCormick had served with him on the board of the Presbyterian Theological Seminary. Southern-born McCormick had opposed the ordination of abolitionists. Horatio had fought his views with vehemence, despite their close friendship.

When another friend, Frances Willard, president of the National Women's Christian Temperance Union, challenged Horatio, he declared he was a strong supporter of temperance.

"Then why don't you join us?" she asked.

"Because," Horatio explained, "you advocate temperance and practice total abstinence."[5]

Even his beloved daughters could not sway his revolutionary opinion that short hair was better for both girls and boys—cleaner, neater, and less bother.

When Horatio's life had flowed like a smooth, tranquil river, he refused to let others shape his course. Now, amidst an ocean of suffering, neither did he bow to their expectations or their theology. Horatio asked his questions of God, not people. He reviewed the Scriptures, wrestled, analyzed, deduced.

"And as Jesus passed by, he saw a man which was blind from his birth. And his disciples asked him, saying, Master, who did sin, this man, or his parents, that he was born blind?" read Horatio. *So, the blind man had his "comforters," even as Anna and I do!* he thought. Horatio read on, "Jesus answered, Neither hath this man sinned, nor his parents: but that the works of God should be made manifest in him" (John 9:1–3).

"God is kind," said Horatio. "I do not know why my children all drowned. But our sin or the lack of it had nothing to do with their deaths. My girls are in heaven. I shall see them again."

He made the long, mournful journey by train to New York with poor Mr. Goodwin, their neighbor, who had lost not only all his children but his wife as well. When Horatio had changed his family's rooms on the *Ville du Havre*, the Goodwins had retained theirs. Horatio later found they were among the first to die in the shipwreck.

"Mr. Spafford, Mr. Goodwin," said the ship's captain. "A word with you, please." When they entered his cabin, he said, with hesitation, "I do not wish to cause you unnecessary anguish, gentlemen. But I believe you would want to know. We have calculated our location with great care, and we believe this is where the *Ville du Havre* sank." He opened his porthole, and the gleam of winter sunshine on the chilly green Atlantic filled the room.

For a moment, neither man spoke. "Thank you, Captain," said Horatio. He and Goodwin left the cabin and by silent common consent, separated. Goodwin wandered to the starboard; Horatio stood alone at the bow of the ship. Three miles deep, the cold, glinting ocean held the skeleton of the *Ville du Havre* and the bodies of his precious little girls.

But you do not hold them, Horatio defied the cruel, unfeeling waves. Tears streamed down his face. *You grasped them for a moment, but my children escaped from this place. Their true Father holds them safe in His arms. Anna and I will see them again, for it is well with their souls.*

Horatio dug into his pocket and pulled out a piece of hotel stationery and a pencil. He began to scrawl words that flowed from his heart in a torrent of pain and faith:

When peace, like a river, attendeth my way,
When sorrows like sea-billows roll,
Whatever my lot, Thou hast taught me to say,
"It is well, it is well with my soul."

Tho' Satan should buffet, tho' trials should come,
Let this blest assurance control,
That Christ hath regarded my helpless estate,
And hath shed His own blood for my soul.

My sin—oh, the bliss of this glorious thought!

My sin—not in part but the whole,
Is nailed to His cross and I bear it no more;
Praise the Lord, praise the Lord, oh, my soul!

And, Lord, haste the day when the faith shall be sight,
The clouds be rolled back as a scroll,
The trump shall resound, and the Lord shall descend—
"Even so—it is well with my soul."

For me, be it Christ, be it Christ hence to live
If Jordan above me shall roll,
No pang shall be mine, for in death as in life
Thou wilt whisper Thy peace to my soul.[6]

Horatio had no idea his daughter Bertha, yet unborn, would one day sing these words to young soldiers of all nationalities in Jerusalem suffering through their last hours of life. He did not know his words would inspire Christians throughout the twentieth century and beyond with their powerful message of God's sovereignty and His great love.

Horatio only knew he could not stop the flow of praise from his own heart as he mourned—and worshipped.

four

Horatio breathed a sigh of relief as he and Anna checked into their London hotel. Anna lay down, exhausted from their journey from Paris. Horatio did not want to sleep; he watched his wife as she sank into deep slumber. Since their sad reunion in France, Horatio wanted little more than to gaze at Anna's translucent cheek, to hold her thin hand in his own like a rosary. Again and again he thanked God for sparing her.

Anna had told him what she knew of the shipwreck. "It was a lovely evening," she said. "The sea was smooth, with no wind to speak of. I put the girls to bed; little Tanetta sang 'In the Sweet Bye and Bye' three or four times before she closed her eyes. She had sung it all day long." Anna's eyes filled with tears. When she could speak, she continued: "About two in the morning, we heard a horrendous noise, like claps of thunder. I knew something terrible had happened. Nicolet [the girls' governess] and I threw blankets around the children and ran up to the deck. An English ship, the *Lochearn*, had collided with us. At first, the captain and sailors assured us the damage was minor; later we heard the *Ville du Havre* had been broken almost in two. No one knows why the ships rammed each other; visibility was perfect that night. Those who might have given us answers were drowned.

"When we realized the ship was sinking rapidly, some tried

to grab life preservers and push lifeboats into the water. But they had been painted and stuck fast to the deck!" The passengers managed to yank a few boats loose and fought desperately to board them. "I, too, wanted to fight for my children's lives!" said Anna, weeping. "But I knew it was wrong to push others aside." Several masts fell on those in the lifeboats, knocking them to their deaths in the freezing ocean. "If I had fought for my rights, as others had, I, too, would have died."

The shivering passengers on the deck had watched the sea rise higher and higher. Maggie, who had been screaming with horror, suddenly quieted. "Mama, God will take care of us," she said.

"Don't be afraid," Annie piped up. "The sea is His, and He made it."[1]

The deck collapsed into the water; the *Ville du Havre* sank only twelve minutes after the initial contact, creating a huge whirlpool. Anna had clung to Tanetta with all her might. The water wrenched the toddler away, but Anna found the edge of her nightgown and seized Tanetta, only to lose her again. "I felt another piece of cloth and grabbed it, but it was corduroy, with a man's leg in it, not my baby."

An athletic passenger had tried to help two of their girls, Anna said. She did not know which two. When she later heard they had almost made it to the lifeboat but lost their grip on their rescuer and drowned, Pastor Lorriaux, who had survived, had to physically restrain Anna from throwing herself into the sea.

"I wanted to die!" said Anna. "I wanted to follow my dear ones! I could not live without them! But God told me, 'You are spared for a purpose. You have work to do.' " Anna remembered Aunty Sims's accusation back at Lake View and decided she would not be God's fair-weather friend. "I will trust Him, and someday I'll understand."[2]

When Horatio and Anna had cried together until they could cry no more, the Spaffords went to the gaily decorated French shops and purchased colorful, expensive toys for a poor pastor friend's children. They sent the surprise Christmas package to the family labeled "from the children."[3]

Expressions of shock, love, and sympathy had poured in from throughout Europe, for which they were grateful. But Horatio and Anna avoided people whenever possible. They did not attend services during Christmas week. Now in London, they would meet Dwight Moody, who was conducting revival services in Edinburgh, Scotland.

The Spafford children always enjoyed Moody's visits to Lake View as if he were a favorite uncle. Annie and Maggie, when quite young, told their parents they wanted to join their church. When the Spaffords discussed it with the evangelist, he considered them far too small to understand such an act. "It would be best to wait a few years," he told them. But when he himself spoke with the girls about Christian beliefs and what their faith involved, he had changed his views. "These children know more than I do. They are quite prepared to join," said Moody.[4]

Now he met with Horatio and Anna in London, so overcome with grief that the bereaved mother found herself comforting *him*. Moody realized the Spaffords were still numb with the shock of losing their family; he anticipated their arrival at the Lake View house might devastate them, particularly Anna, whose life had revolved around Annie, Maggie, Bessie, and Tanetta. Moody's organization had only begun to deal with the needs of poor women in Chicago; if Anna devoted her many talents to helping others, Moody believed both she and his ministry would benefit. "Annie, you must go into my work. You must be so busy helping those who have gone into the depths of despair that you will overcome your own affliction by bringing comfort and salvation to others."[5] Anna agreed to his counsel. The good friends prayed and looked forward to their work together back in Chicago.

Horatio and Anna made their weary journey back to the United States. As Moody predicted, their arrival in Lake View nearly overwhelmed them.

"Oh, Anna, Anna," wept Aunty Sims, who met Horatio and Anna on the threshold of their house. "How could such a thing happen to the dear little girls? What will you do? What will you do?" she wailed. Aunty Sims collapsed into a heap and had to be helped inside the cottage, where she demanded a hot cup of tea.

But Anna, contrary to her usual solicitous nature, stood transfixed. Large portraits of their girls stood on easels in the living room, all bordered with delicate green vines, as was the local funeral custom. Horatio took her arm, and the two ascended the stairs as if in a daze. Upstairs the little beds were made, with toys and books arranged too neatly on the shelves. Starched Sunday frocks hung in the closets, with small nightgowns, delicate chemises, and stockings folded in perfect order. Horatio wanted to close his eyes, but he guided Anna through the house, his hand strong and firm in hers. They wandered into the attic, where a sob caught in Horatio's throat, and he fell to his knees. Four little pairs of rubber boots stood against one wall, with ice skates and sleds lined up in noiseless array. Their friends and family had meant well in their preparations for the Spaffords' arrival at Lake View, but Horatio could not endure this silent monument to his girls' lives.

"We must leave this house," said Anna.

"Let's walk outside," said Horatio.

They made their way down a nearby path in the brilliant late winter sunshine.

"There's the 'post office,' " said Horatio. A ghost of a smile tugged at Anna's lips. The girls had used the hollow trunk of a giant elm tree to leave notes for each other. Now the post office, too, seemed desolate. On impulse, Horatio stuck his hand through the hole in the trunk near the frozen ground. "Here's a letter!" he said, pulling the crumpled, damp paper from its depths. He opened it with trembling fingers; he and Anna read the letter and fell together, their hot tears riddling the snow:

"Good-bye, dear sweet Lake View. I will never see you again."

Maggie Spafford[6]

There's a darkness all round in my earthly affairs,
Wave following wave, tribulation and cares;
My way is shut up on the left and the right;
And yet, I've mind for a song in the night,
A song in the night—a song in the night,
My heart, canst thou give Him a song in the night?[7]

As Horatio struggled to make sense of his children's deaths, he wrote poetry that was published for his friends in a small book, *Waiting for the Morning*. To his surprise, it gained a following; many passed his poetry to grieving family and acquaintances, who demanded more copies. A publisher reprinted *Waiting for the Morning*, and Horatio prayed his writing would help others cope with the unanswerable pain in their lives.

Anna immersed herself in work with Chicago's disadvantaged. To her dismay, Moody appointed her head of women's ministries in his organization. Anna had spent most of her time caring for her husband and family until the Great Fire. She had been a tireless worker in relief efforts, but she enjoyed working one-on-one with women, not running an organization as an executive.

"How can he expect me to make important decisions when I have so little experience?" she asked. Anna then appointed her friend Emma Dryer, another Moody worker, to assist her in day-to-day operations. Emma, efficient and businesslike, helped Anna as a "shadow executive." Later, Anna passed her official position to Emma with true relief. She took far more interest in teaching women to pray at the noonday mothers' meetings she initiated than in formulating budgets.

Anna began to realize what a sheltered life she had led with her children at Lake View. Many women of different ethnic backgrounds struggled with poverty, ignorance, and disease; they often suffered abuse at the hands of husbands who drank to excess when their children were crying of hunger.

When Anna helped convert a prostitute, she found no agencies, Christian or otherwise, who took interest in providing an alternative for the young woman. Incensed, she and Horatio stretched their meager finances a bit further to support the girl until she married several years later.

Horatio continued to run the noontime prayer meetings for men, supporting and participating in YMCA efforts in downtown Chicago, conducting jail services and hospital visitation. Although his own fortune had dwindled, he managed to help Moody build his new tabernacle on Chicago's north side in 1876. He wrote a new hymn, which was sung at the dedication:

> *Our Father, God, Eternal One!*
> *And Thou, the living cornerstone!*
> *And Holy Spirit—one and three—*
> *We dedicate this house to Thee!*
>
> *Take for Thine own, and write in power,*
> *Thy name on wall and shaft and tower;*
> *And make it, by Thy blessing given,*
> *A house of God—a gate of heaven.*[8]

Horatio found himself less concerned than ever with making money. *We do not know how long we will live,* he thought. *How can we devote our precious hours to accumulating riches that can disappear in a moment?*

He and Anna rejoiced when Horatio Goertner Spafford (named after the neighbor child who drowned with their daughters) was born November 16, 1876. Less than two years later on March 24, 1878, Bertha Hedges Spafford also joined their household. Her mother and father named her after Anna's dear friend Bertha Johnson, who had comforted her in Paris after the *Ville du Havre* disaster. They also added the name of their family doctor, with whom they had a special relationship. The little ones did much to heal their parents' wounds with their baby smiles and outstretched, chubby arms. Horatio loved to hold his children close, walking throughout their house, talking to them about their heavenly Father as if he were telling a bedtime story.

When little Horatio was four and Bertha two, their father

took a business trip, knowing Anna planned to take them to see relatives. He hoped Anna and the children would have a good time; perhaps Anna could relax away from Chicago, where their financial situation had worsened. Horatio sighed. *I'll go with them the next time,* he promised himself.

Horatio's business meetings encouraged him, and he felt optimistic. *If things go well, perhaps we can travel to the Holy Land soon.* Years before, Horatio had met a professor who stimulated his interest in Israel and Biblical prophecy. He had always longed to visit Jerusalem and regarded it as the center of God's workings on earth. He dreamed of seeing Bethlehem and sailing with his family on the Sea of Galilee.

"Telegram, Mr. Spafford," said the hotel clerk as he headed for his room to wash before dinner.

Horatio read it and headed for the train station at a dead run.

Anna had returned to Lake View, to Dr. Hedges. Little Horatio and Bertha had contracted scarlet fever.

Horatio threw his arms around his wife and searched their doctor's pitying face. He had come despite a heavy snowstorm and maintained his unceasing vigil.

"Bertha is better," said Dr. Hedges in a soft voice. "But the little boy—"

Horatio closed his eyes.

"He struggles for every breath. He does not respond to anything or anyone," said Dr. Hedges.

In silence, Horatio and Anna went into the nursery. They took turns holding their son until he died before the cold February dawn.

"You want to *what?*" asked Horatio. He could not believe his ears.

Anna stared at their friend, unable to speak.

"I know you have suffered an immense shock," said the man in a gentle voice. "But you have one child left of six; you should do what is best for her."

The Spaffords had prayed with this man and his wife, studied the Bible, sung hymns of worship and thanksgiving, laughed with them many evenings when their Christian group met together. In their hour of renewed pain and suffering, they could not comprehend his suggestion.

He and his wife wanted to adopt Bertha.

"Please leave," said Horatio, fighting the urge to flatten him. "Leave *now*."

"Pray about it," urged the man. He left.

Horatio and Anna sat in silence for some time. The gathering purple winter twilight and the dying fire chilled them, but they did not notice.

"They think we have sinned," said Anna in a flat tone. "Our friends think God has taken our children because we have done wrong. Or perhaps they think we are incapable of tending Bertha—that little Horatio died because I didn't take proper care of him."

Fire exploded in Horatio's head, poured through his veins like molten lava. He tried to keep his voice calm as he put his arm around his wife. "I don't know why they propose to take Bertha, and I don't care what they think. We both know and love God, and He loves us. As for your care of our children, you have devoted your life to them." He touched her pale face.

"I didn't go to Horatio's funeral," said Anna, tears rolling down her cheeks. "Bertha was still so ill—"

"It was enough I was there," said Horatio. Because the Spaffords' house had been quarantined with the outbreak of scarlet fever, few of their friends had known of their son's unexpected death. Fewer still came to the funeral, where Horatio himself read the service as his little boy's white coffin was lowered into the frozen winter soil of the family plot at Graceland Cemetery.

At church, at work—everywhere the Spaffords went—whispered comments and speculations wound around them like deadly tendrils:

"How could a father be so—so unfeeling as to conduct his own son's funeral?"

"Anna is too calm, too pious. She must be near collapse."

"If the Spaffords were true Christians, God would not allow such a thing a second time."

"What will now happen to their youngest, to baby Bertha?"

Horatio and Anna did not understand little Horatio's death any more than they did the drowning of their four precious daughters. Again and again they asked, *Why, God?* No answers materialized. But having suffered through unspeakable tragedy, the father and mother now grasped their faith with a firm hand and clung to God and each other.

Horatio wrote a hymn after his son's death:

Long time I dared not say to Thee
O Lord, work Thou Thy will with me,
But now so plain Thy love I see
I shrink no more from sorrow.

So true, true and faithful is He,
Kind is my Savior;
Alike in gladness and in woe,
I thank Him who hath loved me so.[9]

Anna, too, was determined; she said, "I will say God is love until I believe it!"[10]

The two began making plans to leave the gossips and unfeeling theologians behind, at least for awhile.

"We will go to Jerusalem, where Jesus, the Man of Sorrows, lived," said Horatio. "Perhaps we will find peace there."

five

"A re you all right?" Horatio asked his wife as the rough road grew steeper. He eyed three-year-old Bertha, but she seemed content on the lap of Herbert Clark, the travel representative who had managed their journey.

Anna nodded as she bounced up and down in the "modern" spring wagon lent by friendly Americans living in Jaffa, or Joppa, on the Mediterranean coast. She tightened her grip on baby Grace, who had been born seven months before their departure from Chicago. Anna prayed Grace would sleep through most of the thirty-mile journey to Jerusalem.

Orange groves grew on the dusty hillsides; Mr. and Mrs. Rolla Floyd, who had lent them the wagons, assured Horatio the valleys would erupt with brilliant flowers and delicious fruits and vegetables when the rainy season arrived in a few months. Some grape clusters grew to a length of three or four feet, and apricots abounded everywhere, they said. But Americans from the Midwest could envision no such thing; as they left the small irrigated areas and plodded through the wilderness, the brown, arid hills appeared dead beyond belief.

Desolate or not, Horatio found it all invigorating. *I can see forever! A man can breathe here, follow Christ as his conscience leads him. No more debates with Christians who think misfortune is always caused by sin. No more arguments with those who speak of hell more than they do of God. No more reporters hounding us about our theological stances and writing lurid, lying stories about us.* After his son's death, Horatio had searched the Scriptures, pondered, and challenged his own beliefs and those of others. He questioned Moody's emphasis on eternal punishment and, with his usual openness, shared his opinion that the Bible did not support the concept of a literal hell. When the newspapers heard of the prominent lawyer's stance, they publicized and often distorted his views. One reporter asked Anna if she went into trances and wore cultic symbols. Others asserted Horatio thought he was a second Messiah. One stated the Spaffords and their friends were going to Jerusalem to rebuild ancient ruins and fulfill prophecy.

The elders of Fullerton Avenue Presbyterian Church, which the Spaffords helped build, had asked them to resign their membership.

When many of their friends heard, they also left the church, and soon a fellowship group was meeting at Lake View; some decided to accompany the Spaffords to Jerusalem. Despite the colder weather, Horatio chose to travel a northern sea route to England, rather than France. He did not want Anna to sail past the site of the sinking of the *Ville du Havre.*

Horatio glanced around the wagons at their fellow pilgrims: nineteen-year-old Robert Lawrence, his dead sister Eureka's son; Maggie Lee, another sister; Mrs. William Gould, who had worked with Anna on a committee for the homeless; Mr. and Mrs. John Whiting and their year-old daughter, Ruth; William Rudy, a retired businessman from the East Coast; Caroline Merriman, Rudy's foster mother; Mr. and Mrs. Otis Page and their daughter Flora; Horatio's own daughters' nanny, Nora; and Mr. and Mrs. W. C. Sylvester, who had joined the group upon their arrival in England. *I would not desire anyone's death,* thought Horatio, *but I am thankful we do not have to deal with Aunty Sims.* The loving but needy woman had died before their departure.

When the weary group finally reached Jerusalem, they

stayed in the only European hotel in the city for six weeks while Horatio found suitable housing for everyone. He loved exploring the city, built on four hills, surrounded by walls thirty to seventy-five feet high, constructed in 1542 by the Muslim Suleiman the Magnificent. Jews, Arabs, and Christians—Protestant, Roman Catholic, and Greek Orthodox—crowded together in Jerusalem, which resembled a medieval city, with no electricity and little sanitation. At night, the only lights seen in the unsafe streets were oil lamps carried by the brave.

Horatio watched dark-skinned boys herd goats and sheep through Jerusalem's streets. He smelled the pungent fragrance of *Mo'a lubi*, a layered dish of mutton, rice, pine nuts, and spices, wafting through palm and olive trees. Horatio heard the clink of money as married women, wearing elaborate headdresses of dowry coins under their colorful veils, hurried home from the markets, their cream-colored, brightly bordered robes flapping in the desert breeze. *Do I still live in the year 1881?* he thought.

The American immigrants visited Jesus' tomb, the Wailing Wall, and other Biblical sites. They walked to the top of the Mount of Olives to watch the sun go down in a sea of colors. Horatio lost no time in studying the archaeology so readily available. "This is the land that makes one feel Christ's presence," he wrote.[1] Later, when he and Bertha watched road and sewer improvements dug near their home, he would point to the cobblestones exposed fifteen feet below street level and say, "Look down, Bertha, that is the very pavement our Lord and Saint Paul walked upon."[2]

Horatio found a large white house with stone walls three to five feet thick, with the typical flat roof and dome. "The city looks at a distance like a village of prairie dogs," wrote his nephew Rob in his diary.[3] Horatio also rented two smaller houses and gardens in the same block. He chose this location at the highest point of Jerusalem between the Damascus Gate and Herod's Gate because it presented a magnificent view of the old and new sections of the city. As much as Horatio enjoyed exploring Jerusalem, he could hardly stomach breathing its air, which reeked with animal and human wastes and garbage that filled its narrow streets. *It will be far more healthy up here*, reasoned Horatio.

Several of their group possessed significant wealth; they readily shared their resources with poorer members. Horatio knew everyone would have to pool their talents and energy as well if their community, which was becoming known as the "American Colony," was to succeed.

Anna and the other women enjoyed using native materials as they decorated the big house with rush mat carpeting and bright red material found in markets everywhere in Jerusalem. They accented the light, pleasant rooms with palm branches and bouquets of native grasses. Mulberry, cypress, and pine trees shaded the garden, and luxuriant pink ivy geraniums and white roses climbed to the second story in the courtyard.

The first year in Jerusalem was a difficult one for all as the community members adjusted to the strange languages, foods, customs, and dress of the city's multicultural inhabitants. Their first lonely Christmas was much colder than they had anticipated, with snow and galelike winds that nearly blew Rob off the roof when he attempted to fix their chimney. But three years later, the American Colony entertained thirty-two visitors on Christmas Day, Arabs and Jews alike.

It didn't take us long to make friends, thought Horatio as he spoke first with a Bedouin sheik who had left his tall spear at the door, then two distinguished Jewish rabbis who wanted to discuss certain points of the Law with him. He watched his children, wearing pretty red Christmas dresses, happily greeting their visitors, some clad in European dress, others in Biblical-looking robes and turbans. *Bertha and Grace have flourished here. The rest of us certainly have found little time to become bored.*

Horatio and the other men began teaching English in neighboring schools almost immediately and also tutored Arab and Christian students, giving them an opportunity to meet many prominent Jerusalem families. Horatio never did master Arabic, but his nephew Rob learned it with ease. Rob became his primary interpreter when he conducted daily services and his

47

popular Bible classes at the American Colony and in his frequent trips around the Holy Land.

Anna and the other women held mothers' meetings similar to those in Chicago, and women of all ages, poor and rich, flocked to the big white house to sing, pray, and study the Bible together.

From the beginning, the music at the American Colony drew people of many backgrounds. They loved the hymns and tried to join in the congregational singing, even when they knew little English. The Colony quartet soon became popular; it rapidly grew into a choir. Many in the audience requested African spirituals like "Swing Low, Sweet Chariot" and "Go Down, Moses." Anna's trained voice soared in dramatic solos for audiences she had never anticipated.

"Not the crowned heads of Europe, my dear," teased Horatio, "but certainly a unique and distinguished gathering."

The American Colony's main ministry began one day when the Spaffords took a "picnic tea" on the hillside near their home, as they often did. The friendly Muslim who owned the land came to talk with them while Anna fed baby Grace with a bottle. He had never seen such a thing.

"Perhaps that would help my mother," he said. "She is having difficulty feeding my twin sisters." Anna visited the woman at once and explained through an interpreter how she fed her baby. Anna scoured the markets for the canned milk she believed would be sanitary and nutritious, but could only find Nestle's Condensed Milk. The once-frail twins thrived on their new diet, and word quickly spread that the generous American Colony missionaries had helped the babies. Horatio, Anna, and their friends soon found themselves spending much of their time nursing the sick and teaching hygiene.

"What a pity I am a lawyer, not a doctor," said Horatio.

"Although you have much to learn, you do very well," said Anna, her eyes sparkling.

How good it is to see Anna smile once more, thought Horatio. *I was afraid I would never again see her face light up as it once did.*

The members of the American Colony did not shrink from the unusual number of mentally ill people attracted to Jerusalem. They encountered numerous "prophets," including a man who thought he had discovered the North Pole, and, to their horror, a young girl who blinded herself in an attempt to keep Jesus' commands in the fifth chapter of Matthew. All of these they fed and sheltered unless they posed a direct threat to the other residents of the household.

Both Spaffords enjoyed the frequent visitors at the American Colony. Their Sunday dinner guests might include Islamic clerics or Jewish rabbis, a Russian pilgrim, an English professor, or a Spanish priest, as well as diplomats from the embassies of many countries. Their Arabic visitors smacked their lips to express polite appreciation of their food. Anna tried hard to use kosher cooking methods when their orthodox Jewish friends came to dinner. Often the Spaffords did not speak a guest's language, but Rob's Arabic rescued many a dinner party; their new resident, Jacob, spoke fluent Spanish; and their co-worker Miss Clara Brooke could converse in French or German. Many Jerusalem inhabitants spoke a smattering of several languages, so if plenty of guests were invited, chances were good some diners would understand somebody *some* of the time.

The American Colony grew and established an excellent reputation of Christian hospitality, charity, and compassion.

But it was not without problems.

Because the Colony supplied food, shelter, and clothing, as well as medicine and nursing, to many indigent people, enormous costs mounted steadily. At one time, more than 150 people, many of them helpless or ill, resided at the American Colony. The Spaffords and other well-to-do members of the group soon depleted their financial resources. Horatio's business interests in America suffered because of his absence. Caring friends and relatives often sent monetary gifts to help meet expenses, but the American Colony fell deeper and deeper into debt.

Fortunately, Horatio maintained excellent relations with their Jerusalem neighbors, whose financial help kept the charitable services running. He cautioned their Arab charcoal dealer not to bring charcoal on a regular basis to the Colony because of its lack of funds, but the man ignored him and continued his deliveries, extending credit until Horatio could pay him. Vendors and bankers lent goods and money to the Colony, trusting the Spaffords to pay as they could. Few of their English and American friends in Jerusalem could boast such a rapport with the Arab community.

I wish my Chicago relationships were so positive! sighed Horatio. Before he and Anna had left their Lake View fellowship group for Jerusalem, they had already seen ominous signs of spiritual instability. Horatio had given a stern warning to his friends to avoid dissension and establish strong Christian leadership, but they had ignored him, resulting in spiritual chaos. When the baby of one couple had died, another member refused to allow burial, insisting she would raise it from the dead. The newspapers soon publicized this bizarre scenario, blaming Horatio as the founder of the group. The resulting rumors had dogged the Spaffords for months, even years after their departure from Chicago. Some of their former friends censured the Spaffords in letters to the English Mission and also the United States Consul in Jerusalem. Such criticism damaged the Colony's reputation before it had actually begun, at least in the eyes of the American Consul, Rev. Selah Merrill. At times Rev. Merrill, who held his office a total of eighteen years, used his considerable power to harass the Colony. Some Christian groups, both in America and Jerusalem, regarded the Spaffords and their ministry with suspicion because of their theological differences. Horatio tried to maintain good relationships with as many as possible.

But the Spaffords sometimes found other missions' ministry methods inappropriate. They disapproved of one missionary hospital that forced the sick, even the dying, to listen to an hour of Bible reading in classical Arabic (which few understood), hymn singing, and prayers before they would render any medical care. Anna in particular despised this approach: "Christ would have relieved the suffering with gentle fingers and tender words and allowed the Spirit to do the preaching."[4]

Sometimes other mission groups criticized the American Colony because they believed their Christian community made little or no effort to convert Arabs and Jews.

Horatio himself cherished a deep belief in Jesus Christ. When he heard of a Chicago pastor's sermon disavowing the divinity of Christ, he wrote "Thou Man Divine" in answer:

O Jesus Christ, Thou Man Divine,
'Tis sweet to follow paths of Thine
Where Thou by faith pursuing still
Discerned the Living Father's will.

Faith to Thy heart the time made known,
To lay this world's employments down,
And there at Jordan meet the word
That sealed Thee Son-of-God and Lord.[5]

Horatio refused to pressure people into accepting Christ. But he shared his faith openly as he conducted business for the Colony with merchants and bankers, taught English classes in Jerusalem's schools, or led household prayer services each day. He required all the group, including servants, to attend these.

One eighteen-year-old Muslim worker named Maarouf became so interested in the Bible he decided to become a Christian, though he knew he would face intense family pressures and perhaps even death. When he persisted, Horatio instructed and baptized him, hoping the young man would escape persecution.

But the teen's stepfather would have none of his new religion. He had disgraced his household! He arranged for Maarouf to be conscripted into the Turkish army for five years. One night, as the Colony family sat down to supper, a messenger arrived with a scrap of paper that told his American friends the Turkish military was about to take Maarouf to Damascus. Supper was forgotten in a hurry.

"We must go to the Jaffa Gate!" said Horatio. "We must say good-bye to Maarouf and pray with him!"

The cold-eyed, burly soldiers guarding Maarouf discouraged open prayer. But the Christians gathered around him in quiet love and support. Maarouf would march three hundred miles in excruciating pain, as his hands were tied behind his back by the thumbs, which became infected. When he arrived in Damascus, his captors beat him and subjected him to solitary confinement. But Maarouf refused to deny Christ. They reversed their approach, offering him a lucrative job and a marriage that would guarantee advancement. But he refused all their tactics.

Occasionally Horatio received brief notes from Maarouf that brought tears to his eyes. His young convert put his confidence in Christ and wrote, "I am waiting to the dear Lord for deliverance. Anyway He want it only may I glorify His name in this thing."[6]

One night, years later, the household awakened to a persistent pounding on the front door. Horatio lit an oil lamp, grabbed his stout walking stick, and threw open the door. "Who is it at this time of the night?" he roared.

A filthy, heavily bearded Turkish soldier answered, "I am Maarouf."

He found himself fed, washed, and resting in a clean bed before he knew it. The Colony inhabitants lauded Maarouf as the household hero.

"The children are so happy to see him," said Horatio to Anna. The two smiled as they watched their girls, chattering like little squirrels, bring Maarouf more food than he could possibly eat.

"I hope his stepfather will be content with five years of service," said Horatio.

But the angry man managed to have Maarouf drafted as a *kafir*, an unbeliever forced to serve a lifetime for his rejection of Islam. But two years later the young man escaped from military service in Crete and showed up once more in the American Colony. This time, his stepfather, mother, and siblings all came to visit Maarouf.

"I see now that you have not changed your outer garment

[religion] but it is a change of heart," said his stepfather. "If I work against you, now that I am convinced of this fact, I will be fighting against God. It is written—kismet. I have become your friend, and I respect you."[7]

Horatio bowed his head. *Oh, Lord, may I be a man who loves you as Maarouf does.*

six

A nna, Sheik Fiaz of Heshbon has invited us to visit!" said Horatio.

"Do you think it safe?"

"Of course! He particularly asks that you and the girls come, as many of his people have never seen white women."

Anna gave him a glacial stare.

"It *will* be safe, Anna," insisted her husband. "Sheik Fiaz is sending his warriors to escort us. No one, not even the Turks, dares annoy the Bedouins!" The nomadic people were known for their fierce independence.

Anna smiled. "I know. But—it is so distant, up in the mountains—"

"Where no one can find us! We need a vacation, Anna. You, especially." He touched her thin cheek. With the fresh outbreak of a cholera epidemic in the city, Anna had nursed the sick and dying with little relief. Six-year-old Bertha had been ill with rheumatic fever during the summer, and she had not made a complete recovery.

Grace will fare better here at the Colony, thought Horatio. *But I must remove Anna and Bertha from Jerusalem, at least for a little while.* So one November morning in 1884, a caravan set out from the Colony, guarded by Bedouins laden with swords, knives, and pistols, their flashing black eyes missing nothing. The line of travelers snaked past the Mount of Olives, where Franciscan monks kept brilliant flowers of every color blooming year-round under the gnarled nine-hundred-year-old olive trees. They passed through the peaceful town of Bethany, where Martha, Mary, and Lazarus had entertained Jesus almost two thousand years before, then plodded through desolate hills. When the party paused at a watering place called the Apostle's Fountain, Horatio remained watchful while their camels and horses drank. *I remember all too well the little war that broke out here a few years ago!* The Spaffords and their friends had been enjoying a picnic at the Fountain when rival Bedouin tribes showed up and renewed their feud. *It reminded me of the conflicts over Isaac's wells in the book of Genesis,* thought Horatio, *except that these nomads filled the air with bullets!* But today no other caravan arrived, and their group resumed their slow descent to Jericho as the weather grew hotter.

When Horatio had first arrived in Jerusalem, he realized many of his notions about the Holy Land had sprung from idealized pictures in religious literature. After several years of residing in Palestine, Jericho did not surprise him. Other than several small hotels and a Russian hospice where Greek Orthodox pilgrims often stayed before baptism in the Jordan River, the town consisted of a few miserable huts. He heard Anna's sharp intake of breath at the filth in the streets. "Our friend Abu lives outside the city. I am sure we will enjoy his hospitality."

Abu's home proved pleasant, surrounded by orange, lemon, and banana groves. The caravan halted there that night, then used a primitive ferry to cross the muddy, rushing Jordan. The next day, the Colony group encountered shepherds and their families belonging to Sheik Fiaz's clan. After a refreshing afternoon rest in their tents, the American guests experienced the same dinner they would have had in the days of Abraham: freshly baked flat bread and the "fatted calf," eaten with their fingers from a common dish.

"What are they doing?" asked Anna nervously. The Bedouins

from their caravan had joined the others in a circle by the fire, pulling their swords from their sheaths.

"Some entertainment, my dear, I'm sure." But Horatio's stomach tightened at the sight of the naked blades, and he pulled little Bertha closer.

The black night exploded with wild yells, war songs, the fierce pounding of sandaled feet on the hard, dusty ground. A striking young woman, her drawn sword glittering in the firelight, led the dance, her long, long sleeves flapping in time to her movements.

Did Abraham celebrate like this when he rescued Lot? Horatio wished he could bring every bored Sunday school student to the Holy Land.

When they arrived in Heshbon the next day after a difficult, rocky ascent into the mountains of Moab, Horatio and Anna felt more than ever as if they had been whisked several thousand years back in time. Brawny guards escorted them to the sheik's magnificent tent, 150 feet long and woven of goat hair. Anna and Bertha stayed with the queen, in the women's section, and ate with the sheik's many wives and their handmaidens.

Servants brought Horatio water and washed his feet before he joined Sheik Fiaz, a fat but majestic man who welcomed him as a fellow chieftain. Rich Persian rugs were spread and huge red satin pillows brought, where the Sheik and his closest male family members sat. They motioned for Horatio to join them in the feast: enormous trays of lamb and bread, with bowls of butter and clabbered milk, cakes of raisins, sweets, and strong coffee in tiny cups. Horatio noticed that less prominent household members ate next, then passersby or beggars. No one in the vicinity went hungry. Later the men surrounded the evening fire, and the chief minstrel composed stories and songs about their mighty leader and the fate of the enemies he had conquered. He scattered a handful of dust: "Like grains of dust under his feet, our king's dead enemies cannot be numbered!"

Horatio almost jumped when a female chorus sounded out of the darkness behind him, first on one side of the fire, then the other. As the minstrel continued his story, they echoed the sheik's praises.

This reminds me of the women who sang when David returned from killing Goliath! thought Horatio. He watched uneasily as the warriors' militant passion grew with each song, each story.

But the Beduoin songs, stories, and dances gradually quieted. The women's haunting voices floated out into the cool, rugged mountains, then were lost among the glowing stars.

"Papa! Come! Please, come!"

Horatio looked up from the Colony accounts to see Bertha's wide, troubled eyes. "It's Rob, Papa! He's sick!"

Horatio lost no time in following his daughter to the large room Anna had turned into an infirmary. Twenty-three-year-old Rob, whom they all loved, lay unconscious as Anna sponged his forehead.

"What happened?"

"He was determined to finish surveying and preparing that land at Media for planting trees," said Anna. "His friends said he did not stop, even when the sun was its hottest. Then he collapsed!" Her eyes filled with tears. "He so wanted to help, Horatio!"

"We will pray," he said hoarsely, as he looked at the white, still face. *Oh, God, I lost my only son five years ago. Rob has been like a son to me. Must he die, too?* The fun-loving, brilliant young man who spoke fluent Arabic had had a heart murmur from his childhood, and Horatio feared the worst.

Hours of tender nursing did not awaken Rob, and on September 10, 1885, he died, the first of the American Colony. Horatio and Anna reeled with the loss of their nephew, no less than at losing their five natural children. But tragedy could not dim the faith they possessed, the treasure they refused to surrender.

"We'll see him again, some day," Anna said, her eyes moist but serene.

"Rob is with Christ, along with our other children," Horatio told her. "It is well with his soul—and with ours."

"I wish I could return to Chicago," said Horatio.

Anna knew her husband had just returned from Rob's grave.

Although more than two years had passed since the young man's death, their grief sometimes bled like a fresh wound. "But we cannot escape sorrow by changing our location, Horatio—except when we go to heaven."

"I know." He gave her a sad smile. "But it's more than a mere desire to escape pain, Anna. The Colony continues to accumulate debt. If I could return to Chicago for a year, I believe I could restore our financial stability. Business affairs never prosper without personal supervision."

"I know, dear," said Anna, "but other than money-wise, things are going quite well here. The girls are growing fast and learning so much. Jerusalem is home to them. We have such good friends and would miss them so. I love our work here."

"I do, too." Horatio meant it. Life at the American Colony had proven fascinating and satisfying. He enjoyed caring for the poor and sharing Christ with them. He loved teaching at the Colony and in schools throughout Jerusalem. His friends of many nationalities, economic backgrounds, and religions blessed and challenged him; he believed God used his personal and business relationships to draw them closer to Himself. Horatio would never lose his passion for visiting biblical sites and studying their history and archaeology. He even took an interest in the plant life of his adopted country. He had begun a program of planting fast-growing, hardy eucalyptus trees that he hoped would flourish in the Holy Land, where wood was so scarce.

But Horatio still missed his native land. He had never meant to reside in Jerusalem forever. However, he and Anna knew a trip to America was impossible. Horatio had used the last of their funds to pay for medicines and supplies. "God knows our needs and desires, Anna. If He wants us to go to America, He will provide the means."

"I know." Anna's smile warmed him even more than the steaming bread she offered him. Horatio sat down to rest for the third time that morning. He had not felt well of late; perhaps a long journey was not a good idea. Horatio's sixtieth birthday was fast approaching, and he felt it more than he had expected.

"Let's go camping next week," he said.

Anna brightened. "Do you feel well enough?"

"I need a change of scenery. Too much bookwork, too many worries."

Because Jerusalem had so few hotels, most of its visitors, including the celebrated author Mark Twain, stayed in camps on the hillsides around the city. The Spaffords pitched their tents in a friend's vineyard. They loved the morning aurora behind the hills, the fragrance of sun-warmed vines, the views of the city from high above Jerusalem's crooked streets. Horatio's spirits rose.

But his physical condition deteriorated. Horatio had contracted malaria.

Anna and a servant had to help him up steps when they returned, and Horatio took to his bed. His wife rarely left his side, and all the Colony residents prayed their leader would make a full recovery. But the strong, confident, learned voice of the American Colony faded as Horatio lost consciousness.

"Annie, I have experienced a great joy; I have seen wonderful things," said Horatio, his sunken eyes alight in his white, emaciated face.[1] He struggled to tell his wife and ten-year-old Bertha more about the glory that had filled his room, but his eyes closed once more, and Horatio lapsed into a coma, then died on October 16, 1888.

No hearse existed in Jerusalem, so a lumber wagon carried his rough pine coffin, draped with black cloth and surrounded with pungent pepper tree boughs, down the dusty road to the small American cemetery atop Mount Zion. "Jesus Christ is the resurrection and the life" read the inscription over the cemetery's entrance.[2]

The flames of the Great Fire of 1871 did not shake Horatio Spafford's trust in the sovereignty of his God. The freezing, malignant waters of the Atlantic stole his four little daughters from him, and disease robbed him of his precious little namesake and his beloved nephew, Rob—but nothing could wrest Horatio from his faith in the love of Christ. Poverty threatened to snuff out the light of Horatio's beloved American Colony, but instead, the little lamp multiplied its light and continues to minister to the poor and friendless today in Jerusalem, more than a hundred years later.

Although darkness threatened Horatio Gates Spafford at every turn, his heart sang, "It Is Well with My Soul." Over the years, thousands, even millions, of believers in Christ have learned to sing it with him.

NOTES

Chapter One
1. Bertha Spafford Vester, *Our Jerusalem: An American Family in the Holy City, 1881–1949* (Garden City, N.Y.: Doubleday & Company, Inc., 1950), 11.
2. Ibid.
3. Dwight Moody, *D. L. Moody's Gospel Sermons*, ed. Richard S. Rhodes (Chicago: Rhodes & McClure Publishing Company, 1898), 62.
4. Ibid., 63.

Chapter Two
1. Vester, 3.

Chapter Three
1. Vester, 27.
2. Ibid., 41.
3. Ibid., 40.
4. Ibid., 41.
5. Ibid., 22.
6. Ibid., 45–46.

Chapter Four
1. Vester, 33.
2. Ibid., 36.
3. Ibid., 47.
4. Ibid., 22.
5. Ibid., 48–49.
6. Ibid., 29.
7. Ibid., 51.
8. Ibid.
9. Ibid., 54.
10. Ibid., 55.

Chapter Five
1. Vester, 64.
2. Ibid., 85.
3. Ibid., 65.
4. Ibid., 116.
5. Ibid., 152.
6. Ibid., 73.
7. Ibid., 74.

Chapter Six
1. Vester, 154.
2. Ibid., 155.

Suggested Reading

Moody, Dwight, *D. L. Moody's Gospel Sermons*. Edited by Richard S. Rhodes. Chicago: Rhodes & McClure Publishing Company, 1898.

Spafford Children's Center Association Website. On-line. Cited 25 November 2002. Available from www.spafford-kids.org/history_mission.htm.

Traveling to Jerusalem Website. On-line. Cited 25 November 2002. Available from chass.colostate-pueblo.edu/history/seminar/vester.htm.

Vester, Bertha Spafford, *Our Jerusalem: An American Family in the Holy City, 1881–1949*. Garden City, N.Y.: Doubleday & Company, Inc., 1950.

PHILIP P. BLISS

one

Melodies swirled through the parlor's open window into the freshness of a May morning in 1848. Marches, minuets, sonatinas—Miss Priscilla Fay Birkenstock practiced them all, her slender fingers drawing music from the piano's keys as if by magic. Miss Priscilla paused, picturing the applause she would no doubt enjoy when she performed for the entire village. She rose and gave a gracious bow to her imaginary audience, pondering whether her blue silk dress would set off her blond curls best.

A slight sound broke her reverie. Miss Priscilla raised her head in alarm. A stranger filled the doorway, a ragged boy whose enormous bare feet had left muddy prints on her mother's cherished carpet. Despite his unusual size, she soon realized he was but a child. That fact, plus the dirt, dissolved the scream in her throat. Indignation flushed her pale cheeks.

The boy stared at her with unblinking dark eyes under his shock of dark, wavy hair. "Oh, lady," he said in near worship, "play some more!"

"I will *not*," said Miss Priscilla. "Go out of here with your great feet!"[1]

Ten-year-old Philip Paul Bliss, who had never heard a piano before, left with lowered head and tears in his eyes. But he never forgot the enchantment of the piano, nor the way the young lady had read odd black marks on the pages she turned while she played. Somehow, he had to learn more about this unknown music!

Philip had sung since he learned to talk on the isolated Pennsylvania farm where he was born in a log cabin on July 9, 1838. His father, Isaac, loved to sing hymns on his front porch in the fragrant, rosy light of dawn and in the soft violet twilight after a hard day's work. As a little boy, Philip sat by Isaac and sang with him:

> *Come ye sinners, poor and needy....*
> *Come ye that love the Lord....*
> *Come to that happy land, come, come away....*[2]

"All your favorites start with 'come'!" laughed Philip's mother, Lydia.

"The Lord Jesus wants us to come!" answered Isaac with a smile. The strong, gentle farmer taught his son to whistle and play hymns on homemade instruments. A devout Christian, he enjoyed studying the Bible. Philip and his siblings, Phebe, Reliance, Elizabeth, and James, joined their parents every day for family worship. Years later Philip remembered his father's prayers as "devout, tender, and childlike; repeating over and over again, year after year, about the same words, until we all knew them by heart, his prayers were very real, very holy to me in my childhood."[3]

Philip attended school when he could or learned at home under his mother's daily tutelage.

Although the Bliss family was a harmonious one, they experienced their share of grief and difficulty. Reliance and James both became ill and died when Philip was nine. Continual poverty made it necessary for him to leave home to work on a neighboring farm at age eleven.

Philip carried his clothes bound in a clean kerchief as he started down the muddy path through the forest. His mother could hardly hold back her tears, but Philip smiled and tossed his sisters two pennies he had hoarded for a year. "I'll come visit soon, Ma!" he said and did not look back. Throughout his teen years, he worked on farms or took jobs at lumber camps and sawmills.

At age twelve Philip made a public profession of his Christian faith at a revival meeting. "I've always believed in Jesus and asked Him to forgive my sins," he told the minister. "But now I want to say it out loud." Philip was baptized and became a faithful member of a Baptist church near his school.

He went to school whenever possible. Philip's teachers recognized his superior scholastic ability and his rich bass voice, unusual in a teenaged boy, even one as big and mature-looking as he appeared. A school board in Hartsville, New York, not far from his northern Pennsylvania home, hired him as a teacher in their one-room schoolhouse when he was only eighteen. Philip enjoyed his new job but felt the need of more education. He attended any seminar or training session he could.

When J. G. Towner held a singing school in Towanda, Pennsylvania, Philip decided to go, although he had never before attended one. The young man wandered down the busy main street of the biggest town he had ever seen. Pedestrians seemed to know exactly where they wanted to go and what they would do upon arrival.

Philip removed his old hat and addressed a passerby. "Excuse me, sir. Could you tell me where the Methodist Church is?"

The man frowned, then gave a vague wave in the opposite direction. "Three blocks over. Behind Foster's store." He walked away before Philip could thank him. Philip trudged down the street, wishing he knew one person in Towanda.

Philip found the church and sat as far back in the sanctuary as he could. Stylish young men and women chatted as they waited for the school to begin. *Do they all read music?* Philip had only begun to decipher the puzzling black marks on songbook pages. He looked down at his too-short pant legs and dusty, shabby shoes. *Maybe I better go back home.*

Professor Towner arrived before Philip could exit the sanctuary. He rapped his music stand with a vigorous baton. "Turn to page number one: 'O, for a Thousand Tongues.' "

Philip *had* to stay then; he loved Charles Wesley's hymns, and this one had a good, strong bass line. He forgot about his limited knowledge and poor appearance in his ecstasy in singing the music. He had sung in tiny church choirs, but with such a talented group as this? Never! Even when Towner introduced a hymn Philip did not know, his ear, trained in early childhood, followed its patterns, and he was singing without inhibition by the third verse. After singing school Philip walked back to his boardinghouse in a daze of joy.

"Mr. Bliss," said Professor Towner during their next session. "You appear to have a vigorous voice, just right for this bass solo. Please stand and begin verse two."

The row of pretty sopranos two pews in front of him whispered and tittered. *Are they making fun of me?* But Philip shuffled his big feet and rose, trying to focus on the words of the song. *Please help me, Lord.* To his surprise, he felt his nervousness dissolve, and he poured his heart into the song.

At the end, a stunned silence reigned; then a crash of applause nearly made Philip jump out of his skin.

"Excellent, Mr. Bliss," said Towner. The professor said no more to Philip that night, but by the end of the singing school, they had become good friends. Unknown to either, they would within a few years become singing partners on a concert circuit. Now Professor Towner suggested Philip attend an upcoming musical conference in Rome, Pennsylvania.

"I've heard William Bradbury is leading this convention. Your voice is exceptional, and I'm sure he could help you develop it."

Philip could hardly believe his ears. "Me? I can't even read music yet."

"You're making excellent progress. You need further technical vocal instruction, as well as studies in musical theory," said Towner. William Bradbury, a composer of hymns and Sunday school songs, would later write the music to the song "Jesus Loves Me." He had led choirs of a thousand children in New York City. Philip could hardly believe such a musical giant was coming to Rome, Pennsylvania! Bradbury's influence would saturate Philip's future ministry to Sunday school children.

Convinced he should stay in Rome, Philip procured a teaching position. He began attending a Presbyterian church and singing in the choir.

"That young man's voice is worth a thousand dollars a year. Perhaps he does not know it," said Rev. Darwin Cook, the pastor, to his choir director, O. F. Young, who was also a school board member.

"The boy needs a place to stay," said Young to his wife. He invited Philip to board with them and their five children. All the Youngs sang, and Philip enjoyed the warm, musical atmosphere. Every evening they gathered around the piano and sang popular ditties, as well as hymns and sacred songs. In the Youngs' parlor, Philip practiced the programs he occasionally gave at area gatherings to supplement his meager income. He liked to compose comical pieces and sing them for his eager audience.

"How do you like this one?" asked Philip one evening. He danced a lumbering Irish jig and sang:

Och, bother, shtop yer blarney, just let Ould Ireland shpake;
A blessed darlin' koonthry, too, she is, and no mishtake,
Sich gentlemanly pigs, oh, sich praties there are raised,
Wid niver once a shnake, ye mind, Saint Patrick's name
    be praised!
Ould Ireland, Ould Ireland, Ould Ireland, Hoorah!
Ould Ireland, Ould Ireland, Ould Ireland, Hoorah![4]

The girls shrieked and giggled at the parody, and the two Young boys tried to jig and sing Philip's Irish song with him.

"We'd better quiet our noise," eighteen-year-old Lucy cautioned. "Grandma Allen will soon want to go to sleep."

"I'm sorry," Philip said, abashed. The oldest, Lucy, was a little more reserved than her rambunctious siblings, but now her sweet smile cooled his embarrassment like a fresh drink of water. Philip noted the way the lamplight shone on her wavy dark hair, her white cheek. Lucy's thoughtful, forthright answers in Bible classes at their church impressed him. Her rich alto voice blended so well with his when they sang duets for her grandma. Philip liked all the Youngs, but found himself going to choir rehearsals, spelling bees, and singing schools with Lucy. Soon he could think of little else.

Dare I think of speaking to her of marriage? A teacher hardly makes enough to keep body and soul together. I have fifty dollars to my name! groaned Philip. But one night after singing school, Philip blurted out, "I do so love you, Lucy! Will you marry me?"

She smiled as if she were going to "shush" him, as she did her brothers. But Lucy said, "Yes."

On June 1, 1859, Philip and Lucy drove to a minister's home in Wysocks, a nearby town. There, in his parlor, the young couple exchanged their wedding vows; the fresh joy of the morning smiled upon the new Mr. and Mrs. Bliss as they drove back to her parents' home, where they would live for some time. Philip changed into his rough farmhand clothes, as the chores awaited. Lucy put on a calico work dress and helped her mother cook the evening meal. Little would change, by outward appearances. But Philip wrote in his daily journal entry: "Married to Miss Lucy J. Young, the *very best thing* I could have done."[5]

Philip continued working as a farmhand for his father-in-law for thirteen dollars a month and taught music during the winter at two dollars per evening. The more he taught, the more Philip realized huge gaps existed in his musical knowledge.

If only I could attend more conferences, but they're so expensive! I may as well wish for the moon. . . . I wouldn't trade Lucy for all the music courses in the world. But I wish there were some way I could gain the instruction I need and still support us.

One afternoon when everyone was gone, including Lucy, Philip grew so depressed he threw himself on an old brown settee in the parlor and cried.

"Phil, what is the matter?"

Philip raised his head. Lucy's grandmother stood before him in her shawl and ruffled muslin cap.

"Grandma Allen! I thought you had gone visiting with the others."

The old woman's eyes twinkled. "I told them I was too tired to go visit Hattie Mae Anderson. And so I am. I'm too tired to listen to her go on and on about her aches and pains, which are no worse than anybody else's."

Philip grinned through his tears.

"But I'm not too tired to hear why you're so troubled." Grandma sat down and rocked in silence. The measured *thump-thump* of her rocker calmed Philip. He handed Grandma a program for the upcoming Normal Academy of Music in Geneseo, New York, 1860.

"So, you're a-wantin' to go to this school—is that right?"

"Yes, Grandma. Look at the instructor list: Perkins, Cook, Bassini—some of the best teachers there are! But it costs thirty dollars; that's more than I make in two months."

"Well, thirty dollars is a good deal of money." She paused in her rocking. "I have an old stocking that I have been dropping pieces of silver in for a good many years, and I'll just see how much there is. Perhaps there are thirty dollars, and if there are, why, you can take it and go to the Normal."[6]

Philip threw his arms around the old lady, speechless.

She laughed. "What kind of school would it be without its best student?"

Philip went to the Normal Academy for six weeks, inhaling musical knowledge like oxygen. *Thank You, God. I'll make You and Grandma proud.*

Armed with his new skills, Philip began his music teaching career in earnest the winter of 1860. His father-in-law supplied him with the necessary equipment. "Old Fanny (a horse) and a twenty-dollar melodeon [a small organ] furnished by O. F. Young set me up in the profession," Philip said later.[7]

For three years he combined teaching, farming, and education whenever he could. Philip attended the Normal Academy again in 1861, then in 1863. Sometimes he had to leave Lucy at her parents' farm while attending classes. "A pleasant winter," he wrote a friend, "only my wife, Lou, was at home; so I was only half a man, *if half.*"[8]

Philip wrote his first song, "Lora Vale," and sent it to William Bradbury, hoping he would recommend it for publication. Although the song spoke of the dying girl's going to heaven, it was more in a popular vein than religious:

> *And beyond the silver moonbeams,*
> *Aye, beyond the stars of night,*
> *Now she dwells, our darling Lora,*
> *In the home of angels bright.*[9]

Bradbury rejected "Lora Vale."

"Don't worry," Lucy consoled her husband as he sat, downcast, at supper. "Mr. Bradbury composes Sunday school music; 'Lora Vale' isn't what he publishes. Someone will realize what a good song it is! You just wait and see!"

As usual, Lucy was right. In 1865 Root & Cady Music Company published "Lora Vale."

"Root & Cady out of Chicago!" said Philip as he leafed through the mail his friend James McGranahan gave him. James, a fine tenor and fellow musician, made his living working as a general store and post office clerk. He read the publisher's name on Philip's envelope and gave a low whistle. He could not resist teasing his friend and snatched the envelope from Philip.

"Give it back!" said Philip, laughing but annoyed.

"Not unless you open it here so I can read it, too!" said James, stuffing the letter under the post office counter.

"You're holding up United States mail, McGranahan."

"Throw me in jail."

Philip sighed. "Lucy will forgive me for opening it before I come home. If Root & Cady are rejecting the song, too, I guess it's just as well." James tossed him the letter; both young men held their breath as Philip read its contents.

He threw his hat into the air and whooped at the top of his voice. James let out a loud "Hurray!" and shook his friend's hand until Philip thought it would fall off. The loafers dozing on benches outside squinted, then exchanged glances. Crazy musicians!

"My friend, the composer!" said James, grinning from ear to ear. He himself had published two songs, and he understood what Philip was experiencing!

"I thought Mr. Root had forgotten me," said Philip, shaking his head in wonder. "We had excellent conversations at the last music conference, but I never expected such a kind response to my letters since. And I certainly didn't expect this! I know it's only a proof; but my song, in *print!*" He stared as if he could not believe his good fortune. Philip bowed his head for a brief moment. "Thanks be to God for all His good gifts."

"Amen," said James.

"I'm going to need your help making corrections," said Philip, looking askance at the store's owner, who had stopped working in the back room to grin at their antics.

"It's not long 'til closin'. Go ahead and celebrate, boys!" said old Mr. Harris. "But you'd better take this with you." He gave Philip a package.

"From Root & Cady, too!" Philip tore it apart and found a flute in its case. "Our compliments to an excellent musician," read the card. Overwhelmed, Philip could hardly keep tears back.

Mr. Harris handed Philip a bag of horehound candy. "Take it home to your Lucy, Phil."

"Thank you!" Philip's eyes shone. *We'll have such a celebration tonight! Lucy and her family have done so much for me.* Aloud he said, "Come to dinner, James. Grandma Allen's making chicken pie this evening."

"I'd never refuse an offer like that," said James, who slept in a room above the store and subsisted mostly on hardtack and salt pork.

Later, after they had dissected "Lora Vale," the two young

men made their way down the road to the Young farm, sucking candy sticks like schoolboys. Neither Philip nor James dreamed both would one day sing and compose gospel music for audiences throughout the United States and even across the sea.

two

"We're not holding up our end," said Philip. "The money from our concerts doesn't cover our salaries, let alone our expenses."

"With such hard times, what can we expect?" said J. G. Towner.

With the end of the Civil War, the Root & Cady Company had hired Philip and his former teacher to publicize their music, singing in concerts throughout the North. The publishers did not reproach the "Yankee Boys" for their lack of income, but both singers disliked creating a deficit. Too, Philip had grown weary of months of travel and constant time away from Lucy.

"I may as well be in the army," said Philip.

"Be thankful Lee surrendered right after you were drafted," said Towner.

"I am! But I think I'm done with concert tours after this one," said Philip.

Both resigned, and Towner pursued other musical paths. But Root & Cady asked Philip to remain with their company for a guaranteed salary of $150 per month plus expenses. "We need someone to hold conferences, sing in concerts, and teach our new music in churches," said George Root. "We are also interested in your composition talents." Philip liked the arrangement far better, as Lucy traveled with him. But he grew disgruntled when his intake the first year did not match his salary.

"One hundred dollars will be sufficient income for us until Root & Cady make a profit from my work," said Philip stubbornly. Root agreed but raised his salary the next year, as Philip's teaching conferences, called "normals," began to draw hundreds who wanted to learn music under their gifted leader.

During his ten years of association with Root & Cady publishers, Philip's talent for composition not only met but surpassed their expectations. "I do not know of his modes or habits of composition," wrote George Root later, "but [I] do know of his wonderful fertility and facility. His responses to the calls for the many kinds of literary and musical work that we soon found he could do always surprised us as much by their promptness as by their uniform excellence. It is probable that with every topic that entered his mind there came trooping multitudes of congruous ideas, images, and words, and he had only to take his choice. . . ."[1] Root & Cady, as well as other publishers, grew to appreciate Philip's prolific, flawless music manuscripts, which he recopied rather than submit with erasures. He wrote and edited his first collection of hymns and Sunday school songs called *The Triumph* in 1868. Many of Philip's songs were included in *The Prize*, a collection of Sunday school songs edited by George Root himself in 1870.

According to an article he wrote for Root & Cady's musical journal, *Song Messenger*, Philip and his friends enjoyed a unique rehearsal of *The Prize*'s new songs on their first train tour to publicize the hymnal: "We drew out a thousand miles of music from *The Prize* last week, coming from Chicago. There was also an opposition quartet, led by a Buffalo editor, accompanied by spotted pasteboards and a wicker demijohn [whiskey/wine bottle]. Supported by some ministerial and musical friends, we opened on them such batteries as 'The Armor of Light,' 'Immanuel's Land,' 'There's a Light in the Valley,' etc., which soon compelled them to beat an ignominious retreat, taking their demijohn, but leaving a visible odor of poor tobacco and worse whisky."[2]

Philip contributed many articles to *Song Messenger*, as well as other journals of music, under the pseudonym "Pro Phundo Basso." Sometimes he satirized the conventions and normals he conducted. He loved poking fun at self-important musicians who had forgotten the sheer joy of singing.

Philip also wrote popular sheet music during this early period of his career—sentimental favorites like " 'Tis the Heart Makes the Home," "The Woodbird's Song," and "Little Lou," which he wrote for his wife:

> *And to-day with my darling here beside me,*
> *With her loving heart, so noble, kind and true,*
> *I can battle with the sorrows that betide me,*
> *For the sake of my loving little Lou.*[3]

Others were more thoughtful, such as "Farewell, Old Year"; "Boys Wanted," which urged boys to set worthy goals; and "The Last Bugle":

> *Farewell, brother soldier, in peace may you rest,*
> *And light lie the turf on each mouldering breast,*
> *Until that review when the souls of the brave*
> *Shall behold their chief ensign, fair mercy's flag wave.*[4]

Philip sometimes sang for Union Temperance meetings and wrote "Look Not upon the Wine" and "The Temperance Ship" in support of the movement. He wrote a friend: "I believe in women, prayer, and God; so there's only one side for me in the great crusade."[5]

Many of Philip's secular songs, however, gave a smile to singers and hearers alike, with his renditions of "Aunt Tabitha's Trials," "A Tragical Tail," and "The Photograph":

> *A pretty picture, really;*
> *I'd know if I shall see,*

But if 'tis very pretty, why,
It can't look much like me.[6]

Lucy helped Philip at his conferences, sang alto in occasional duets, and worked at Root & Cady's store in downtown Chicago between tours. During summers, the Blisses often returned to Rome, Pennsylvania. Philip believed the peaceful countryside inspired his writing more than Chicago.

But they occasionally had to remain in the city because of business. One summer evening in 1869, Philip and Lucy decided to walk downtown, hoping Lake Michigan's breezes would refresh them.

"It can't be hotter than it is in the house," said Lucy, fanning herself.

Philip and Lucy made their way past families sitting on their steps and front porches as the sun went down. Philip took Lucy to their favorite ice cream parlor, where they sipped lemonade in frosty glasses. Then they wandered through the gathering dusk.

"What's going on?" Philip pointed to a crowd of people gathering around the courthouse. "An accident?"

"I don't see any damaged wagons or hear horses," said Lucy. "I think they're listening to that man at the top of the steps."

"I know him! It's Dwight Moody, the shoe salesman turned preacher!" said Philip.

Lucy sniffed.

"Now, Lucy, he's a good man from all I've heard—one who cares for people who don't know Christ," said Philip.

"There are so many charlatans! They debase the name of Christ with their greed and deception," said his wife with disgust.

"I want nothing to do with them," agreed Philip, "but I believe Moody is different. Come, let's go listen."

Dwight L. Moody read from a worn Bible in a voice that could be heard by all, "Then said he unto him, A certain man made a great supper, and bade many: And sent his servant at supper time to say to them that were bidden, Come; for all things are now ready. And they all with one consent began to make excuse" (Luke 14:16–18). The young evangelist mopped his forehead and took a step forward with a smile. Philip felt as if Moody were about to shake his hand.

"Now, I venture to say that if I should go down among the congregation here tonight, every man that has not accepted this invitation would be ready with an excuse. You have all got excuses. You would have one right on the end of your tongue. You would be ready to meet me the moment I got to you. If I met that excuse, then you would get another, and you would hide behind that. . . . And so you would go on, hiding behind some excuse. . .and if you should get cornered up and could not think of one, Satan would be there to help you make one. That has been his business for the past six thousand years. . . . Excuses are the cradle, in other words, that Satan rocks men off to sleep in."[7]

Philip expected someone to heckle the earnest preacher in the long, shabby frock coat. Instead, respectful silence reigned, and when Moody invited the crowd to hear him in Wood's Museum at the corner of Randolph and Clark streets, they followed him there like a flock of sheep.

Philip hurried to procure a seat for Lucy as people pressed into the auditorium. Sweat poured down his face. *This religious meeting smells more like a gymnasium!* he thought. But Philip paid little heed to the oppressive heat. He could hardly wait to hear Moody speak again.

Before the evangelist preached, a song leader mounted the stage and led the group in several hymns. The man flailed the air with weak, random motions, like a bird with a broken wing. He confused the words of the songs. He occasionally drifted off-key, which sent chills up Philip's spine. Philip stopped singing and closed his eyes. *Lord, I think the song leader is doing his best, but please deliver us!* He heard Lucy's clear alto beside him and felt ashamed. *I'm sorry, Lord; You are worthy to be praised, no matter what.* Philip took a deep breath and followed the song leader. Voices around him, encouraged, followed his powerful bass and by the end of the song service, most were singing the right verse to the right tune.

Moody once more held them all spellbound. Philip could not remember when he had so enjoyed a sermon. *See the number of people who have come forward to give their lives to Jesus Christ!* Philip forgot about the musical famine at the beginning of the service.

But Moody had not. "Welcome!" he said, giving Philip's hand a vigorous shake. "Thank you for rescuing us during the hymns!"

"Was I that loud?" asked Philip, his face crimson.

The evangelist laughed like a boy. "Yes, quite loud!" he said, then lowered his voice. "Thank God you were loud! My regular song leader could not be present this evening. Albert is a fine, willing Christian, and he's a better song leader than I am but not by much!" His eyes twinkled. "Do you live here in the city?"

Later, as the Blisses walked home, Philip realized he had volunteered to lead Sunday evening song services whenever he was in Chicago—which would be often, as he was writing more and more for Root & Cady.

"Where have you been hiding Bliss for four years?" Moody asked Philip's employers, who were friends. "Sending him out of town to sing for everyone else! How is it no one in Chicago has heard him?"

"Dwight speaks well of you, Mr. Bliss," said Major Daniel Whittle, a volunteer evangelist who often worked with Moody. When he could not book Philip's current duet partner, C. M. Wyman, to lead the music for a Sunday school convention, he had asked Moody's recommendation for the position.

"What a singer!" he told Moody after the conference. "No meeting can languish when Philip Bliss leads the song service!" Whittle became a lifelong friend and future biographer. One of his messages inspired Philip to write his most popular song. In 1870 Major Whittle preached about a Civil War incident in which General Sherman told a faltering group of Union soldiers to "Hold the fort!" Inspired, Philip went home and wrote out the entire hymn by the same name, as well as its music, as he often did. "Hold the Fort!" caught the imagination of the post-Civil War North and spread throughout music conferences and churches in the United States, even emerging as an international favorite:

Fierce and long the battle rages,
 But our Help is near;
Onward comes our Great Commander
 Cheer, my comrades, cheer!

"Hold the fort, for I am coming,"
 Jesus signals still.
Wave the answer back to heaven,
 —"By thy grace, we will." [8]

Major Whittle suggested Philip to the pastor of the First Congregational Church in Chicago as a music director candidate. Philip and Lucy spent three happy years there, living with the Whittles for some months, whose home was located only a block from the church. Philip Paul Bliss Jr., whom they called Paul, was born in 1872, to the delight of their church family. Little George Goodwin Bliss, named after their pastor, would arrive in 1874.

When Philip directed the choir, he stood before a large red cross that dominated the stained glass window. "I am glad we have the cross always before us," he told them. "Let us forget everything else when we sing. Let us seek to have the people lose sight of us, of our efforts, our skill, and think only of Him who died thereon, and of the peace, comfort, strength, [and] joy He gives them that trust Him."[9]

His powerful voice never allowed mediocrity in a service. Dr. E. P. Goodwin, his pastor, said when a prayer service grew "listless and stupid," Philip "would break out at such times with one of his ringing songs that would go through all hearts like the blast of a bugle, and set everything astir."[10] Philip held strong opinions about congregational singing: "Every meeting for God's worship should be a praise meeting. . . . Many a good sermon has been blown away for want of a hearty hymn to harrow it in. Many a poor prayer meeting has dragged its slow length along for want of the lubrication of a cheerful praise-spirit manifested in some soulful song."[11]

He had no patience with lukewarm renditions of hymns sung by a thoughtless congregation: "Let us remember, when we stand up in the congregation to sing, that we are either singing to the Lord or (is it possible?) taking His name in vain!"[12]

"How many sermons do you remember from your child-hood?" asked Philip of those who shrugged at the spiritual value of music. "How many songs do you recall?" Above all, sincerity in faith should be modeled and taught to the young, Philip told the adult members of his congregation. No wonder children were not sincere in their worship when they saw adults shuffling through pages or staring about the church, eyes glazed with boredom, while singing "Nearer, My God to Thee."

Not long after Philip became the music director of the Congregational Church, he also took on the job of Sunday school superintendent, and his compositions reflected his growing interest in children. He wrote songs like "Dare to Be a Daniel" and "Jesus Loves Even Me," which achieved the national and international success of "Hold the Fort." In 1873 he wrote and edited a Sunday school hymnal, *The Sunshine.*

"You may have a flower garden without a fountain, a parlor without pictures, or a summer day without the sunshine; but do not expect a wide-awake, stirring, effective Sunday school—a school that shall enjoy a healthful popularity, and be in the highest sense successful, without Sunday school singing. . . . Therefore, we are not here to meet the question, 'Shall the children sing?' but to suggest *what* and *how*."[13]

Philip urged song leaders to ask children what their Sunday school songs meant. He himself, as a child, thought "prone to wander" meant "a long-legged fowl wandering in a swamp." "Fearless, I'll launch away," young Philip had believed, involved an all-important subject: lunch![14] Such memories inspired the adult choir director to insist, "Help children to worship with their hearts *and* heads."

Philip planned children's Sunday school music to reinforce the Bible lessons he taught them. He deplored the insertion of random songs for no good reason and advised against the use of heavy hymns for little ones. And while some Sunday school song leaders encouraged children to "Sing loud!" to the point of screaming, Philip declared this damaged young voices and did little to promote spirituality. "Earnestness is not always best manifested by loudness. Noise is not always power," he said.[15]

Philip's sense of fun endeared him to children. He received many letters from them when he visited churches or held conferences in their area. Philip wrote one little boy, Charlie, who asked if a true Christian could have fun: "I was. . .full of fun when I was a boy. Mrs. Bliss says I have not gotten over it yet. I do love fun, and love to romp and play with my little boys. . . . I love my friends and music very much, but that does not prevent my loving Jesus. No, I think I love Him all the more for giving me so many pleasant things and a cheerful, happy heart."[16] Philip loved answering the children's questions and spending time with them. When any in his Sunday school were ill, he visited them.

One day, when Philip and Lucy were Christmas shopping, he saw a small, shabby girl staring at dolls in a shop window, the longing naked on her pinched little face. He could not help himself: "Now, just pick out the one that you want, and you shall have it," he told the child. "I will go in and buy it for you." The little girl stared at him in terror and ran away as he pled with her. Saddened, he told congregations later, "That is just the way sinners treat Christ. I was real grieved that the little one wouldn't let me do for her what I wanted to, and that she distrusted me, when I just wished with all my heart to make her happy. I think I understand a little better how the Lord feels at our unbelief of His precious promises."[17]

Many children responded to Philip's love and devotion with commitments to Jesus Christ. When adults doubted the genuineness of their conversions, Philip pointed to Jesus' attitude toward little ones: "Jesus welcomed children into His arms. Shall we do otherwise?"

Meanwhile, Moody and Ira Sankey were holding meetings in England, beginning with a congregation of four, which quickly grew to thousands. British audiences had never heard such hymns in religious meetings; their typical services had included only the formal singing of psalms. When Sankey led one of Philip's light, joyous songs, they responded to Moody's invitation in droves. The Britishers loved "Jesus Loves Even Me." Sankey also taught "Hold the Fort!" to his eager revival audiences. For a time, it was the most popular religious song sung in the United States and Britain and was eventually translated into Zulu, Chinese, and some Indian languages. Englishmen bought thousands of penny copies of the words and wanted more lively new hymns.

"We need Bliss here in England!" said Moody. He wrote Philip many times while overseas, urging him to resign from his business commitments and "sing the Gospel."[18]

Philip agonized. "I love the work I do," he told Lucy. "It's God's work. But is He changing my direction? Does He want me to travel as a singing evangelist?" He held his head in his hands. "Moody asks me to take an uncertain way, with no real assurance of income. After all our lean years, I so want to buy you a house of your own."

Lucy had rarely complained about their lack of a home and their frequent extended stays with friends, relatives, and strangers. She adjusted to Philip's erratic work schedules, creating a pleasant atmosphere wherever they went. She and Philip had saved for years and had just begun to look for their dream house.

"If we go to England for months, who will care for Paul and little George?" Philip adored his sons; he wrote friends that Paul was "the blessedest child, fat and healthy, good-natured as—as—his *paw*,—that's me!"[19] When little George arrived, he wrote a poem, "Georgie's Welcome," which his still-close friend, James McGranahan, now a director of Root's Normal Musical

Institute, set to music. "I can hardly bear the thought of not seeing the boys for a year or more. And, Lucy—" his eyes grew deep with intensity—"Lucy, I can't consider such a life without you. God did not bring us together to separate for such a long time! I will not accept it. I cannot."

She touched his head. "Pray, Phil," she said softly. "God will show you the correct choice. But it should be God's choice, not man's."

Lucy told a friend, "I am willing that Mr. Bliss should do anything that we can be sure is the Lord's will, and I can trust the Lord to provide for us, but I don't want him to take such a step simply on Mr. Moody's will."[20] Unlike some of Dwight Moody's followers, practical, shrewd Lucy did not regard the colorful evangelist as infallible.

Philip prayed and pondered his motives. Perhaps he was letting his own joy in performance and travel carry him away. Did he care more about seeing Europe than helping people find Christ? Was he overestimating his own abilities?

Moody wrote him: "You have not faith. If you haven't faith of your own on this matter, start out on my faith. Launch out into the deep."[21]

The evangelist was also sending persuasive letters to Major Whittle, pleading with him to come to England and preach. Major Whittle and Philip shared their reservations about such a bold endeavor, debating the pros and cons. They prayed together and encouraged each other. Lucy was relieved her husband had such a partner in decision making.

Their quandary was interrupted by a close friend's tragedy. Horatio Spafford and his family had lived next door to the Whittles at one time. The influential lawyer and tireless Christian worker received word his four daughters had perished in a terrible shipwreck on their way to Europe. Major Whittle walked the floor with the devastated father all night. The Blisses had grown to love the Spaffords almost as much as the Whittles did. They all cried with Horatio, prayed with him, and sent him on his way to France to comfort his grieving wife. While sailing past the location where his children drowned, Horatio penned the magnificent hymn "It Is Well with My Soul." When he returned from Europe in 1874, still mourning but resolute in his faith, he showed the poem to Philip, whose eyes overflowed with tears.

"Horatio, God has given you these words," said Philip.

"I could not speak them unless He had," answered Horatio. He sat in silence, his gaunt face weary and drawn.

"Should God grant me the melody, may I set your poem to music?" asked Philip.

His friend nodded, a smile warming his sad, dark eyes. "I was hoping you would, Phil. Perhaps in hearing it, some suffering soul will cling to the Savior." He dug through his valise and handed a letter to Philip. "I almost forgot! I spoke with Mr. Moody while I was in England, and he asked me to relay a message to you and Major Whittle."

"I can guess its content," said Philip. He skimmed the letter.

"He wants you and the Major to come evangelize England?" asked Horatio.

"Of course! 'Hasten! Christ calls you to England!' "

"I am persuaded," said Horatio slowly, "that no one can interpret the will of God for anyone, save himself."

"I will take the letter to the Major," said Philip. "We will continue to pray together about this."

"Both of us have served as evangelists," said Major Whittle when the two met. "But my business still occupies most of my time, as do your conferences and ties with Root & Cady and other publishers."

"Perhaps we should conduct more meetings together here in the United States before we consider England," said Philip. "If God blesses our combined full-time efforts and people come to Christ here, I would feel more positive about working overseas."

For the hundredth time, Philip and the Major prayed God would communicate His plan for them.

One day when the two were riding a train to a Sunday school

conference, they encountered a pastor, Rev. C. M. Saunders of Waukegan, Illinois. Their "small talk" deepened into a conversation about their mutual concern for people without Christ. By the time they entered the train station, Philip and Major Whittle had agreed to a three-day revival in the pastor's hometown in March. They went back to Chicago and prayed. "If God draws sinners to Himself in these Waukegan meetings," said Philip, "let us agree to give up other pursuits for this noble one—that of helping the lost find Him." The Major acquiesced.

The time for their departure arrived, and the two waved good-bye to their wives as the train chugged out of the station.

"Do you think our experiment will work?" asked the Major.

"We'll soon find out," answered Philip. He had stood before congregations for years and thought "butterflies" were a thing of the past—evidently not.

To Philip's relief, he found Rev. Saunders had honored his request by providing an organ and recruiting choir members from area churches. He had asked for plenty of kerosene lamps throughout the sanctuary; their glow reminded Philip of the Holy Spirit's fire. *The Major and I are not alone in this endeavor. Show us Your plan, O God.*

Evidently God's plan did not include an initially large turnout. The enthusiastic but sparse congregation included staunch Christians from a few area churches. When the sullen skies poured icy rain the next day, Philip was sure their numbers would diminish to nothing that night.

"Well, we wanted a sure answer from God," said Major Whittle, trying to smile.

To their surprise, twice as many people attended. At the end of the service, several approached the altar, giving or dedicating their lives to Jesus Christ anew. When everyone else had gone home, Philip and the Major met for several hours at the Congregational Church to pray.

"I'll give up the conferences, Jesus, if You want," Philip said. "I give You my secular music writing, my sacred writing. I place my life at Your disposal, for any purpose You design."

The next night, twenty people came to Christ! After the meeting, Philip and Major Whittle looked at each other in silent agreement. When they returned to Chicago, Philip began to contact replacements to fill out his conference schedule; Major Whittle resigned from the Elgin Watch Company. The two began to make plans for more evangelistic meetings together.

three

Home tonight. Home tonight! Philip's heart composed its own song of joy in time to the chuff-chuff of the train. He and Major Whittle had just finished a series of meetings in Wisconsin. Again and again they had seen people pray, oblivious to their friends and neighbors around them, as they responded to the Major's messages and Philip's songs. He had sung his hymn "Almost Persuaded" in closing the last service, and men, women, and children had given their lives to Christ:

> *"Almost persuaded," now to believe;*
> *"Almost persuaded," Christ to receive.*
> *Seems now some soul to say,*
> *"Go, Spirit, go Thy way,*
> *Some more convenient day*
> *On thee I'll call."*[1]

To think a song of mine could play a part in their salvation! Thank You, Lord!

Ira Sankey had once told Philip about an attorney who had come to Christ as the congregation sang "Almost Persuaded" at the end of the meeting: "I am not only 'almost' but 'altogether persuaded' to put my trust in Jesus Christ!"[2]

"Phil, I think 'Almost Persuaded' has helped convert more people than any song you've written!" said Sankey.[3]

Home tonight! Home tonight! Philip praised God for the wonderful results of their meetings. Since he and the Major had become full-time evangelists, Philip had written his friend James McGranahan several times, urging him to leave his work with music conferences and use his talents to bring the lost to Christ. As the train rumbled through cities and fields, Philip skimmed James's last letter. His friend told him once more he did not think he had the aptitude for full-time evangelism and chided Philip good-naturedly for his persistence: "You sound just like Moody!"

Philip grinned, then rubbed his aching head. He loved his work, but he was weary as he watched the snow-laden trees fly past his window. *1876. A new year. Already?* During the past two years, he and Major Whittle had led services throughout Kentucky, Tennessee, Missouri, Alabama, Georgia, Pennsylvania, and Illinois, as well as in the upper Midwest. Philip's friendship with the Major had warmed, ripened as they shared the joys and trials of working together. Their success had recently precipitated more talk of Europe.

Their revival schedule had grown so heavy that Philip had resigned his position at the First Congregational Church. His choir had surprised him and Lucy with a lovely farewell gift: a silver monogrammed tea and coffee set. Fighting tears, Philip joked, "If I'd known I'd get such a fine present, I might have resigned before!"[4]

He missed his friends in Chicago, but more than anything he wanted to be with Lucy. *Not many women would endure what she does,* thought Philip. He had written his mother: "My time is so taken up with the meetings, going and seeing, etc., while she is left with the monotonous, everyday duties of home life, and that almost like yours, a widow. But nevertheless, the Lord has given her a cheerful heart, and she is just as content and reconciled as anyone could be; says she would not detain me if she could and prays, oh so earnestly, for my success and safety."[5]

She has not reproached me because we do not possess what we could.

Lucy had written a friend, "We have not much that is elegant here now, but we have the most 'magnificent inelegance,' that the world has ever known."[6]

God has blessed me with a wonderful wife. And the boys! Paul changes every time I see him. And Georgie is into everything. Philip chuckled. The last time he was home, the toddler had climbed into the coal box and emerged black as tar.

Philip and Major Whittle would have to leave again for meetings in St. Louis at the end of the month. But until then, Philip intended to spend every moment he could with his family.

Chuff-chuff-chuff-chuff! The train sped through the countryside, faster and faster. Philip's heartbeat increased with it. *I can't reach Chicago fast enough.*

Philip's last year, 1876, would be one of his best. Major Whittle remembered Philip's increased Christian maturity at 38, his joy in the conversion of friends for whom he had prayed, his flourishing music ministry in which he wrote and published songs such as "My Redeemer." Even his travels took him places he longed to see, and Lucy accompanied him on his evangelistic tours with Major Whittle while their boys remained in Chicago with friends or stayed with their families in Pennsylvania.

The Blisses especially enjoyed their March trip to meetings in Alabama. They took a train to Vicksburg, Mississippi, then rode a steamboat along the Mississippi River to New Orleans. Philip and Lucy marveled at the mile-wide expanse of muddy water as it eddied and flowed.

"Is it safe?" asked Lucy. She heard deckhands talk of spring floods of past years.

"Not very," teased Philip.

She retorted, "Perhaps you need to spend more time in prayer, anyway."

They boarded a train to Mobile, Alabama, marveling at clouds of creamy pink magnolias and peach blossoms, the green leaves budding everywhere.

"I didn't know March could be so beautiful!" marveled Philip.

"Not much like Chicago!" laughed Lucy. "Where are the freezing winds off Lake Michigan, the sleet, the snow?"

"Far, far away, thank God!" answered Philip. He squeezed his wife's hand. "I'm so glad I can share this with you."

"Everyone in the South has been most kind," said Lucy, with a little hesitation.

Philip knew his wife had feared their reception, and he shared her concerns. After all, they were Yankees, visiting an area still wounded and bleeding from the Civil War only a decade before. "The Major and I encountered some hostility in our earlier southern meetings," he answered truthfully. "But we've also met opposition in other places besides the South. Remember the Missouri Medical College in St. Louis? Those boys imitated Whittle and me, 'preaching' and singing gospel songs with the most unholy lyrics. But eventually they listened to us, and many came to Christ. Most southern people have welcomed us as their brothers and sisters in Him. God will take care of us, Lucy."

She smiled and nodded. "As He always has."

When they arrived in Mobile, the Christian mayor of the town gave them a public welcome. The area pastors had already met and collaborated in organizing the meetings. Lucy's fears dissolved as large, attentive audiences responded to the gospel in record numbers. Young men and women who packed a Baptist church in special Sunday afternoon meetings gave their lives to Jesus Christ with a fervency that brought unspeakable joy to Philip. He conducted one Sunday evening service for men at the Mobile Opera House, where he sang his songs "Pull for the Shore," "What Shall the Harvest Be?" and tender, family-oriented songs like "Memories of Childhood" and "Trundle Bed." Almost two hundred men accepted Jesus Christ that night!

After ten days, the evangelistic team departed for Montgomery, where authorities permitted them to hold meetings in the City Hall. Again, large numbers attended and responded to the gospel.

Separate services were conducted for African-Americans in both Mobile and Montgomery. Major Whittle also remembered "arrangements made for their attending the general meetings."[7]

Philip reveled in their passionate singing and unashamed emotion in their worship, and "their wild and plaintive melodies."[8] "I wish we were all as open in our adoration of the Lord as they," he told Lucy. The African-Americans' favorite Bliss song was "Father, I'm Tired," and Philip could barely refrain from weeping when he thought of all they had endured as slaves and the difficult life they still led.

The group next traveled to Selma, Alabama, where the Young Men's Christian Organization, founded only five years before, brought their boundless enthusiasm to the meetings. They had cleaned and prepared a huge cotton warehouse for the services. Choirs from various churches had practiced songs they hoped would grasp the hearts of their hearers. Large crowds of teenagers and young adults came to the warehouse to listen and give their lives to Jesus Christ.

Lucy returned to Chicago to make arrangements for their usual summer stay in Pennsylvania. Philip and Major Whittle traveled on to Augusta, Georgia, where at a beautiful Easter morning service on the courthouse square, Philip sang his song "Hallelujah, He Is Risen" before a crowd of three to four thousand worshippers. They then went to Rome, Georgia, and on to Marietta.

"Let's go to Kennesaw Mountain," suggested Major Whittle, "and see the place of the battle that inspired your song "Hold the Fort."

"Do we have time?" Philip could only think of all the work he had to do.

"I think it's important," answered the Major.

So the two left Marietta and rode by carriage the two miles to Kennesaw Mountain. The sun shone as if glad that winter was gone. Large mats of purple and white violets bloomed beside the road. The old horse drawing their hired buggy whinnied as if the morning air had made him young.

"What a day!" marveled Major Whittle. "It's hard to believe not ten years ago, hundreds of men lost their lives near here." They stopped the carriage and climbed to the top of Kennesaw.

Altoona Mountain, where the outnumbered soldiers of an important Union fort made a valiant stand against overwhelming Confederate forces, lay to the north twenty miles away. General Sherman and his relief troops had rushed to their aid, signaling with flags from the large, grassy valley between Kennesaw and Altoona, "Hold the fort; I am coming!"

"It is a testimony to the bravery of the soldiers," said Philip. "They followed their commander's orders to the end! And we must do the same." He fumbled with his Bible. "I want to read some Scripture. 'Let us hold fast the profession of our faith without wavering; (for he is faithful that promised;) And let us consider one another to provoke unto love and to good works. . . . Cast not away therefore your confidence, which hath great recompence of reward. For ye have need of patience, that, after ye have done the will of God, ye might receive the promise. For yet a little while, and he that shall come will come, and will not tarry' " (Hebrews 10:23–24, 35–37). Philip closed his Bible and searched the brilliant blue sky. "Do you see Jesus yet, Major?"

"Not yet," answered the evangelist, "but soon."

"Perhaps in our next breath," answered Philip. He sank to his knees. Major Whittle followed, and the two prayed, giving their energy, talents, and love to Christ anew. Philip sang "Hold the Fort" until the melody cascaded through the surrounding hills, as if sung by an angel army:

> *Ho, my comrades, see the signal*
> *Waving in the sky;*
> *Reinforcements now appearing,*
> *Victory is nigh.*

> *"Hold the fort, for I am coming!"*
> *Jesus signals still,*
> *Wave the answer back to heaven,*
> *—"By Thy grace we will."*[9]

"I thank my heavenly Father that I was led to so urge my

friend and brother to make that mountain visit," wrote Major Whittle later. "He reckoned it, while he lived, as one of his blessed days, and the memory of it to me is, and will continue to be while life lasts, a transfiguration scene."[10]

four

"Bills paid, publishers' meetings done, books boxed, papers filed and packed, furniture hauled to storage—what else should I do?" Philip asked Lucy. He and his wife were packing their belongings, as they planned to remain in Pennsylvania with their families the rest of the year.

Weary, she pushed a tendril of dark hair from her forehead. "I have a thousand details to attend to," she said.

"I will take the boys to the park," said Philip.

"Let's go!" said Paul, his eyes dancing in his thin, pale face.

"Do you think he is well enough?" began Lucy, as the little boy tried to put on his shoes. Their four year old had been very ill for several weeks.

"The fresh air and sunshine will do him—and you—good," answered Philip. Two-year-old Georgie crowed with delight as he tossed him into the air. He turned to his grateful wife. "It will not be long, my dear. We will soon be with your family, and you will get some much-needed rest."

In Pennsylvania the O. F. Young family welcomed the Blisses, exclaiming over the boys. Lucy, her mother, and sisters caught up on family news, and Philip enjoyed doing farm chores. "I spend so much time in the city," he said. He sang as he pitched hay for the plowhorses and fed the placid cows.

He and Lucy took several side trips that summer. They visited the Philadelphia Exposition and Chautauqua Lake, New York.

"What a crowd!" said Philip as they disembarked from the steamboat that had carried them from their hotel across Chautauqua Lake to Fair Point, where Philip was to sing. Everywhere the Blisses looked, they saw tents and crude huts with laundry and hammocks strung between trees. Families emerged. Mothers in light summer dresses carried parasols and picnic baskets and herded little children in bathing dress toward the beach. Men and boys played three hole catch, a forerunner of baseball, and discussed the latest camp meeting preacher or temperance speaker.

"Lewis Miller and John Vincent opened this Normal only a few years ago," said Philip.

"I thought it was mostly for Sunday school teachers," said Lucy.

"It was, the first year. Now they're inviting other Christians to come and learn, too. This year they're offering classes on Greek and Hebrew and conference meetings about Sunday school and family topics. I've heard they're even planning classes and games for children!"

"Perhaps we can bring the boys in a year or two," said Lucy. The Blisses enjoyed the free-and-easy atmosphere. Philip and Lucy found the classes relaxed but stimulating, as Dr. Vincent believed education was for everyone and endeavored to engage the best teachers. Later, Chautauqua became a famous conference and entertainment center, a model for many "chautauquas" throughout the United States.

"So delightful to spend time with other Christians. We can study, dine, swim, and go boating on the lake; no saloons or profanity to disturb us, as in Chicago," said Lucy.

"They finished a temperance convention here a few days ago," mused Philip. "Perhaps that is why the crowds are so big."

The next evening Philip sang at the "auditorium," which consisted of rows and rows of rude benches under the trees. But hundreds of people fanned themselves and sat enrapt as Philip's powerful bass echoed across Chautauqua Lake, where the first stars glimmered in the sky and the smooth water:

"Let the lower lights be burning!
Send a gleam across the wave;
Some poor, fainting, struggling seaman
You may rescue, you may save."[1]

President Rutherford B. Hayes's wife, Lucy, had requested Philip's song "Let the Lower Lights Be Burning" when the Columbus Glee Club sang for her. Philip rejoiced his hymn was sung in the White House. But he reminded himself to keep his focus on Christ. "Pray for me," he had told a pastor friend, "that success may not be a temptation to me."[2]

Philip and Lucy enjoyed Chautauqua Lake, then took a train to Massachusetts, as Moody and Ira Sankey, who had returned from Europe, were holding meetings in the Boston area. Moody lost no time in including Philip and Lucy in his week's schedule. They traveled more than a hundred miles through the hills of Vermont, New Hampshire, and Massachusetts, helping Moody with eleven meetings!

"Not exactly a vacation," said Lucy to her husband with a smile.

"We both knew Mr. Moody makes a habit of drawing his visitors into whatever he's doing," said Philip, shaking his head.

On the long rides between meetings, he and the evangelist discussed the trip to England again. "Can't you see God has blessed your meetings with Major Whittle?" asked Moody. "Hundreds of people will live in heaven forever because of your songs, your leadership, your testimony. Nothing is more important than this!"

"God has seen fit to work through us," answered Philip. "But the Major and I must pray and discuss this once more before we give you a final answer."

Moody did not nag Philip, but he could not help saying at their parting, "England is waiting for laborers, my friend. England is white unto harvest!"

Philip and Lucy returned to Rome, where Paul and Georgie greeted them with exuberant hugs. Paul made sure his parents knew he had worked hard every day, hunting eggs in the henhouse.

After a few pleasant weeks, the Blisses knew they must return to Chicago. Philip joined Ira Sankey at the Pacific Hotel for two weeks in October as they worked on *Gospel Hymns No. 2*. The two had collaborated mainly by mail in their other efforts. Now they could create together, playing the organ, singing, and praying. Sometimes tears ran down their faces as they worshipped together. Other times the room rang as they collapsed in laughter over some musical joke or lyrics that would never grace Mr. Moody's meetings.

"I have never before experienced such friendship with a dear Christian brother of like mind," said Philip.

In November Philip and Lucy went to Kalamazoo, Michigan, to perform at the Baptist College and the young women's seminary, then to Jackson, Michigan, for more meetings. As usual, they found opportunities to pray with several people who needed spiritual counsel: a minister's daughter who could not believe in the Jesus she had heard about all her life; a wealthy young couple, well-known in their community, yet without God; an elderly man bedfast for seven years, treated to a personal concert by Philip; a cynical telegraph operator who came to meetings because he liked Philip's singing, although he refused to believe the gospel.

"Jesus cared for individual people," said Philip. "Concerts and meetings are all very well, but some lost ones need more."

He sang in several churches in Jackson, but also went to the Michigan State Prison, where he spoke and sang to eight hundred prisoners. Philip talked to them about their wives and little ones waiting for them, and about his own children, Paul and Georgie, whom he missed every day. Philip said he would never have sent his son Paul to die a terrible death for his enemies. "Oh, friends, I could not do it, but this is what God did for you. He loved you and gave His Son to die for you."[3] When Philip sang his hymn "Hallelujah, What a Savior," his voice ringing throughout the prison, many tough, cynical prisoners sat with bowed heads, trying to stifle their tears:

> *"Man of sorrows!" what a name*
> *For the Son of God, who came*
> *Ruined sinners to reclaim—*
> *Hallelujah! what a Savior!"* [4]

Philip and Lucy returned to Chicago, where he sang a hymn he had composed weeks before, "Are Your Windows Open Toward Jerusalem?" for a thousand pastors at Moody's Christian Convention. *I remember when Horatio Spafford led a service at the state prison in Joliet,* thought Philip as he sang warm-up scales in the church basement. *Horatio preached on Daniel, and his words moved me until I had to write the song:*

> *Do not fear to tread the fiery furnace,*
>   *Nor shrink the lion's den to share;*
> *For the God of Daniel will deliver,*
>   *He will send His angel there.*

> *Are your windows open toward Jerusalem,*
>   *Though as captives here a "little while" we stay?*
> *For the coming of the King in His glory,*
>   *Are you watching day by day?* [5]

"Amen!" chorused many of the pastors who listened. "God bless Mr. Bliss for that song!" called one.[6] Dwight L. Moody sat in silence, overwhelmed as he meditated on the words of the hymn.

It was the last time on earth they would hear Philip sing.

five

R ev. Morgan from London will arrive in a week," said Major Whittle. "Are we going to England with him?"

Philip, Lucy, and the Major were spending Thanksgiving with good friends in Peoria, Illinois. They had discussed the British revival meetings once more and prayed together.

"I have lost my passion for work in the Chicago area," said Philip. "Instead, I want to go to New England, where Mr. Moody has been preaching. If all goes well, I will go to England with him. Lucy will accompany me."

"We think it best Paul and Georgie remain with my sister Clara; it will not be a big adjustment for them, as they have spent so much time with her already and love her like a mama. Constant travel and life in a foreign country would not be good for them. And I would be free to help Philip in the meetings," said Lucy.

"If you are drowned on the way to England," said one acquaintance, "at least the children would not perish."

Philip, Lucy, and the Major sat in silence, remembering Horatio Spafford's tragic loss three years before.

"I hadn't thought of that," answered Lucy slowly. "If we ask the Lord to guide us, and it seems best for all to go, and we are all drowned, it is all right. . . . We should all go together."[1]

Philip took her hand. "God will take care of us."

"See you in Chicago on New Year's Eve!" said Major Whittle.

Philip winced. "I do not know why Mr. Moody believes it necessary for me to return here," he said. "After I spend Christmas with my family in Rome, why should I travel all the way back to Chicago? Logically, I should remain there until we leave for England. Or at least I should stay on the East Coast. I do not understand his reasoning, but I will return to sing on December 31, if I receive his confirmation."

"Don't worry about it. Enjoy your time with your children," said Major Whittle.

Philip smiled. "I plan to."

What a Christmas it was! Philip and Lucy had loaded a trunk with presents for Paul and Georgie and their extended families. Philip cut down a large evergreen and dragged it to the Youngs' farmhouse, setting it up in the parlor. He and Lucy sang Christmas carols as they hung gift after gift upon the Christmas tree. Philip dressed in a bright red suit the next day and played Santa Claus to the entire family. His little boys did not recognize their papa behind the white beard, although Paul regarded him with suspicion when Philip forgot his disguise and sang "Hark, the Herald Angels Sing!"

"Thank you, Santa," said Grandma Allen as Philip handed her a brightly wrapped gift. The old lady could scarcely rise from her chair now, but her eyes shone as keen as ever. Philip planted a kiss on her wrinkled cheek. "I should thank *you*, Grandma," he whispered. "Again and again!"

Full of joy, Philip celebrated the Christmas season by visiting old friends and relatives and inviting them to receive the God whose love sent His only Son to earth as a helpless baby. "Why, that man would come in and say, 'Grandma, I wish I could see every person in this valley a Christian,' " Lucy's grandmother said later.[2]

When he did not receive Moody's confirmation of his singing date in Chicago after Christmas, Philip wrote Major Whittle, saying, "Unless I hear from you, I shall not leave this week."[3]

"He [Philip] had been advertised to sing in Mr. Moody's

102

Tabernacle the following Sunday afternoon," the Major wrote later. "It was necessary to telegraph him to come. But evening came and found me at my home and the telegram was not sent. I had not forgotten it but did not want to send it. I did not know then, I do not know now, why. All day long, it was upon my mind and was spoken of to friends that Bliss must be telegraphed for, and that I did not like to take the responsibility of doing it. Late in the evening, the dispatch was forwarded."[4]

Philip accepted the telegram the next morning after breakfast; he read it and sighed.

"We must leave for Chicago?" asked Lucy.

"Yes, Lou. As it is already Thursday, I had hoped Moody would change his mind. But I suppose I'd better go buy the train tickets. I do not think we should take Georgie and Paul. This will be their home while we are in England, and they should be uprooted as little as possible. I will tell the boys we're leaving."

"I suppose I should pack," said Lucy. Neither moved. They both gave a rueful laugh. "It's been such a *lovely* holiday here at home," said Lucy.

"I know." Philip straightened and rose. "But now it is time to be about God's business." A scream erupted from the nursery. Philip chuckled and went to investigate. With great care, Paul had lined up his new tin soldiers for battle. With similar precision, Georgie was knocking them down.

"Boys, boys," soothed Philip. He grabbed Georgie and held him on his lap, then helped Paul rearrange his battalion. They played together, then Philip explained he and their mother were leaving for Chicago later that afternoon and would return soon. "I would love to stay. I would far rather stay than go, if it were God's will; but I must be about the Master's work," said Philip.[5] "Now, boys, let's pray."

Paul bowed his head; he had grown accustomed to this ceremony before his parents left for meetings. Little George folded his chubby hands, still clutching one of Paul's soldiers. Philip spoke a fervent prayer, then hugged them both. *Thank You, God, for two beautiful, healthy sons who are learning to know You.* He glanced at Paul's rosy cheeks. No trace of illness now, thank God! *The boys are Your best gifts to Lou and me.*

After saying their good-byes, Philip and Lucy made a chilly trip to the Waverly train station in O. F. Young's wagon. "What time will you make Buffalo?" asked Lucy's father.

"About midnight, if all goes well," answered Philip. "There we'll change trains; we'll take the Lake Shore and should arrive in Chicago Friday evening, with sufficient time to rest before Sunday."

But all did not go well. Engine trouble delayed their train to Buffalo and forced the Blisses to take a later train. Instead of riding all night, they decided to stop overnight at a hotel in Hornellsville and take a Friday train to Buffalo, where they would connect with the Lake Shore.

"I'd better telegraph Whittle that we'll arrive at nine o'clock Saturday morning, rather than Friday night," said Philip irritably.

"Perhaps we will be less exhausted because of our stop," said Lucy.

"At least our luggage will make it to Chicago on time," said Philip, trying to laugh. He had checked their big trunk straight through. They arrived without further incident at Buffalo but had to wait, as the Lake Shore train was an hour late.

Clouds of gnat-like snowflakes assailed them as they boarded. "I think it's growing colder," said Lucy, stamping her feet.

"Wind's picking up," observed Philip. "Glad we're not traveling in a covered wagon this afternoon!"

They made their way down train aisles to the parlor car and sat down, grateful for the glowing stove and the comfort of kerosene lamps brightening the gloomy afternoon. Several couples and two families with children settled into nearby seats, and Philip lost no time in making friends with the little boy and girl sitting across from them.

"Philip Bliss! I didn't know you were on my train," said a dapper-looking businessman.

"Good to see you!" answered Philip with a smile. He had met J. E. Burchell at one of his conferences years ago, and they had kept in touch. The two chatted about Philip's plans to go to England with Dwight Moody.

"Terrible weather! I hope it doesn't delay us much more," said Burchell as he tipped his hat to Lucy and headed for his own car.

"A good afternoon to read the Scriptures!" said Philip, smiling, as he opened his Bible.

The train pulled out of the station, then increased its speed to fifteen miles an hour.

Philip opened one eye. The train seemed to be chugging at a slower pace than earlier. Lucy had fallen asleep, her dark head bent over her knitting. *We should both head for the sleeper soon. No sense in staying up.* He could see nothing but darkness and whirling torrents of snow through the train windows. *Getting worse. I hope we don't have to stop for the night.* Philip straightened his tie. The little boy and his sister had also given in to sleep. Their peaceful faces reminded Philip of Georgie and Paul.

Suddenly the train car gave a sharp lurch to the right, then the left, like a pendulum swung at the end of a chain. *Crack! Crack!*

"Lucy! Lou!"

He made a frantic grab for his wife, but could not find her in the tangle of arms and legs where he found himself. The fancy ironwork in the car twisted into grotesque snakes of grinding metal as kerosene lamps sailed off tables. Philip heard screams, the smashing of glass, and the howl of the savage wind as the train car plunged seventy feet into unknown darkness.

"Have you heard from Lucy's parents?" asked Dwight Moody, his face white and tense.

"Nothing," answered Major Whittle. Upon reading the *Chicago Tribune*'s account of a train accident in Ashtabula, Ohio, Saturday morning, he sent an immediate telegram to Pennsylvania. He knew Philip and Lucy had planned to leave on a later train, but the weather had no doubt wreaked havoc with schedules. Had they indeed left Rome? If so, which trains had they taken? After sending the dispatch, Major Whittle banged on Moody's door and told him of the accident. The two began a vigil that grew darker with each passing hour of silence.

"God is with Philip," said Moody. "Although the Blisses are delayed, we will no doubt receive a message soon to meet them at the station. We will give thanks together again and again for their safe return!"

"May it be so," said the Major. "God is with them." But he could not dispel the foreboding in his heart, even as he and Moody offered fervent prayers for Philip, Lucy, and their sons, as no one in Chicago knew Paul and Georgie had remained in Pennsylvania. Periodically Major Whittle went to the train station for information. He heard only reports about the wreck and confirmed Philip and Lucy had not ridden the train that arrived Saturday afternoon from Buffalo.

At three o'clock that afternoon, a telegram arrived. "Thank God!" said Moody, tearing it open.

Oh, Lord, let them be safe, prayed Major Whittle. *Please, Lord. Please!*

A stranger to the evangelist, a man named J. E. Burchell, had sent the telegram. He had survived the train wreck at Ashtabula. Thirty-eight-year-old Philip Bliss, whom Burchell had recognized from Sunday school conferences, did not.

"We were to have heard Philip sing today. . . ," said Major Whittle. His words trailed off in tears. Others from Moody Tabernacle who had accompanied him to Ashtabula wept.

James McGranahan, who had also traveled to the site of the accident, said nothing, too grieved to speak.

They stood at the top of the ravine, looking down at the mangled, melted remains of the train cars partially submerged in the frozen creek. The broken bridge gaped like an open wound.

Major Whittle mourned not only his friend, but their common cause. *Who will now sing God's truth in England? Who will go with me to rescue sinners?* His eyes fell upon James McGranahan. Only a week before, Philip had discussed James's exceptional musical talent with him. *Here stands the man that Mr. Bliss has chosen his successor.*[6] The thought burned into the Major's mind. He could not know James McGranahan would join him for eleven years in revivals in Great Britain and the United States or that the two would collaborate to produce such songs as "Showers of Blessing" and "I Know Whom I Have Believed." But a tiny ray of light pierced Major Whittle's dark depression as he surveyed the ugly scene.

Rescue workers fought their way through waist-deep snow, hoping to recover bodies and clothing, bags, jewelry, cuff links—anything to help them identify the victims. Piles of white ash covered the smoldering ruins. More than a hundred passengers had perished in the accident. Several days would pass before Philip's friends realized Paul and Georgie were safe with their grandparents.

"Terrible, terrible fire," said the Major, closing his eyes in pain. "I doubt they will find much."

Later, Philip's friend Burchell confirmed his fears in his eye-witness account of the accident: "All had escaped alive, though all were bruised or injured. The fire stole swiftly along the wreck, and in a few moments the cars were all in flames. . .from out the frozen valley came great bursts of flame. There were crowds of men there, but the fire beat them back, and they could do nothing. . . . The fire crept steadily on through the snow flakes, leaping from one mass of ruins to another, licking up the blood as it passed along, and crushing out human lives as remorselessly as it curled around the stubborn woodwork."[7]

After a three-day search, including dragging the bottom of the creek, the workers found no remains of the Blisses. Only their large trunk, filled with music, had made the journey safely to Chicago.

"Know ye not that a prince and a great man is fallen this day in Israel?" cried Moody to his congregation the Sunday after the wreck. The evangelist struggled to gain his composure as he surveyed the crowded, silent sanctuary, draped with mourning and the four crowns of white camellias and lilies placed on the altar.

"Who shall take the place of this sweet singer, and carry on his noble work for Christ? It seems as if this consecrated voice and pen could not be spared, as if they had hardly crossed the threshold of their mission for the good of men and the glory of God."[8]

The entire nation echoed his grief for Philip and Lucy. Churches throughout the Midwest and the South held memorial services for the Blisses, in addition to those conducted in Moody Tabernacle and Rome, Pennsylvania. Sunday school children in many states who had sung Philip's songs and loved his lessons collected $9,500 in pennies to pay for his gravestone and to support the orphaned Paul and Georgie.

"Only thirty-eight years old!" said Moody to Major Whittle. "It seems the Master could have left him with us a little longer, to bring more souls to Christ!"

Many Christians struggled with the same emotion. In his short life, Philip had written hundreds of gospel songs, sung to thousands, and talked at length with cynical fellow travelers, fidgeting Sunday school boys, troubled students, depressed invalids, and hardened prisoners about Jesus Christ. At one point his song royalties generated sixty thousand dollars, yet he refused to buy a house, devoting the funds instead to caring for the poor.

Why had God allowed him to die so young, so tragically?

Philip's last hymn, "He Knows," found among his papers not long after the accident, answered the pain of those who loved him best:

> *So on I go, not knowing,*
> *   I would not if I might;*
> *I'd rather walk in the dark with God*
> *   Than go alone in the light;*
> *I'd rather walk by faith with Him*
> *   Than go alone by sight.*[9]

NOTES

Chapter One
1. Daniel W. Whittle, *Memoirs of Philip P. Bliss* (New York, Chicago, and New Orleans: A. S. Barnes & Company, 1877), 18.
2. Ibid., 16.
3. Ibid.
4. Ibid., 207.
5. Ibid., 22.
6. Ibid., 23–24.
7. Ibid., 24.
8. Ibid., 26.
9. Ibid., 31.

Chapter Two
1. Whittle, 33.
2. Ibid., 221.
3. Ibid., 199.
4. Ibid., 195.
5. Ibid., 257.
6. Ibid., 200.
7. Dwight Moody, *D. L. Moody's Gospel Sermons*, ed. Richard S. Rhodes (Chicago: Rhodes & McClure Publishing Company, 1898), 77–78.
8. Whittle, 70.
9. Ibid., 45.
10. Ibid.
11. Ibid., 227.
12. Ibid., 224–225.
13. Ibid., 222.
14. Ibid., 223.
15. Ibid.
16. Ibid., 191.
17. Ibid., 53.
18. Ibid., 49.
19. Ibid., 241.
20. Ibid., 49.
21. Ibid.

Chapter Three
1. Whittle, 139
2. Ibid., 178.
3. Ibid., 169.

4. Ibid., 241.
5. Ibid., 246.
6. Ibid., 236.
7. Ibid., 67.
8. Ibid.
9. Ibid., 304.
10. Ibid., 68.

Chapter Four
1. Whittle, 114.
2. Ibid., 186.
3. Ibid., 80.
4. Ibid., 81.
5. Ibid., 83–84.
6. Ibid., 83.

Chapter Five
1. Whittle, 86.
2. Ibid., 92.
3. Ibid., 93.
4. Ibid.
5. Ibid.
6. J. H. Hall, *Biography of Gospel Song and Hymn Writers* (New York: Fleming H. Revell Company, 1914; reprint, New York: AMS Press, Inc., 1971), 193 (page citation is to the reprint edition).
7. Whittle, 294–295.
8. Ibid., 328.
9. Ibid., 367.

Suggested Reading

Hall, J. H., *Biography of Gospel Song and Hymn Writers.* New York: Fleming H. Revell Company, 1914. Reprint, New York: AMS Press, Inc., 1971.

Moody, Dwight., *D. L. Moody's Gospel Sermons.* Edited by Richard S. Rhodes. Chicago: Rhodes & McClure Publishing Company, 1898.

P. P. Bliss Home Page. On-line. Cited 25 November 2002. Available from gbgm-umc.org/DesertFoothillsAZ/PPBLISS.

Town of Busti History Website. On-line. Cited 5 April 2003. Available from www.townofbusti.com/chaut_lake.html.

Whittle, Daniel W., *Memoirs of Philip P. Bliss.* New York, Chicago, and New Orleans: A. S. Barnes & Company, 1877.

WILLIAM COWPER

one

enjamin Franklin shivered and drew closer to the crackling fire. The May evening seemed more like early March. Franklin had visited Great Britain several times before Congress had chosen him to help negotiate peace after the Revolutionary War. However, British weather, with its endless clammy fogs and mists, seemed to affect him more now. *But then, I am seventy-six years old, and the slightest chill freezes my bones.* His eyes wandered to a new book in his bookcase, entitled *Poems*, which an old friend had sent him as a gift.

Franklin had responded with a groan. "Most poetry is for lovesick young fools, not old men like me who have seen too much!" he told his very proper housekeeper, Mrs. Stout.

But now, a week later on a dreary evening when Franklin's aches and pains troubled him too much to go out or receive company, he opened the little volume by William Cowper and began to read. Soon he could not stop.

He read "Conversation," a poem about Cowper's discussion with a loud, ignorant man:

> *Vociferated logic kills me quite,*
> *A noisy man is always in the right,*

Useless in him alike both brain and speech,
Fate having placed all truth above his reach,
His ambiguities his total sum,
He might as well be blind, and deaf, and dumb.

Their own defect, invisible to them,
Seen in another, they at once condemn;
And, though self-idolised in every case,
Hate their own likeness in a brother's face.[1]

"He must have dined with the same fool I did this Sunday past," said Franklin to the fire. Captivated, he finished the book in two sittings, then penned a note to his friend, thanking him for the gift: "The relish for reading of poetry had long since left me; but there is something so new in the manner, so easy, and yet so correct in the language, so clear in the expression, yet concise, and so just in the sentiment, that I have read the whole with great pleasure, and some of the pieces more than once."[2]

I've heard Cowper has written a hymn book with John Newton as well, thought Franklin. *Hymnals rarely interest me, but I will buy that one.*

Later that year Benjamin Franklin roared with laughter as he heard John Henderson, an actor, read a sixty-three-stanza comic ballad called "The Diverting History of John Gilpin." All England loved the story about a hapless businessman who tried to celebrate his wedding anniversary but found himself on a runaway horse, chased by upright citizens who thought him a thief. Franklin bought a copy of the text, whooping and chortling as he read it:

Away went Gilpin, neck or nought;
Away went hat and wig,
He little dreamt when he set out
Of running such a rig![3]

Mrs. Stout poked her head through the library door and

bestowed a dark frown on his uninhibited merriment. Franklin grinned at her icy disapproval, but quieted.

They say Cowper wrote "John Gilpin," but that he does not wish others to know it, mused Franklin, chuckling as he reread his book. *Perhaps he considers it inferior because it entertains, rather than moralizes. The poem is clever and refreshing and bears his unmistakable stamp, despite its lightness. I wonder what Cowper will write next? Whatever it is, I must take a copy back to America with me.*

About the same time the American statesman Franklin read "John Gilpin," all England discovered the genius of fifty-year-old William Cowper, a writer who had penned numerous hymn texts and other poetry throughout his devout but troubled life.

William was born November 15, 1731, in Great Berkhamstead, Hertfordshire, the son of Rev. John Cowper, who served as chaplain to King George II. His mother, Anne, was descended from John Donne, the English poet. His three older siblings had not survived; Anne, although drained from her hard delivery, now saw with delight her baby boy was strong and healthy.

"Praise be to God," she murmured, holding the infant close. He let out a squall, and she nursed him, grateful for his vigorous hunger. "William. . .Willie? Or Will?" The baby stopped to look at her with liquid eyes. "May you grow to love God all your life," Anne prayed as she caressed his soft baby cheek.

Little Will adored Anne throughout his early childhood. When she died in childbirth with his brother John five years later, the child could not stop crying. Future medical authorities would point to Anne Cowper's death as the traumatic event that profoundly impacted William's spiritual and literary life. His father, kind but distant, could not cope with his sensitive little boy's intense grief. At age six, William found himself on his way to boarding school. The gloomy, dark buildings, the chilly dormitory where he slept with many strange boys, most older than he, only made the child weep without pause.

"For shame! Such a baby!"

William raised his head from his hard pillow. In the shadowy moonlight, the Boy loomed over his bed, a mutant giant. William could not see his face, but he could feel the cruel grin, the scornful eyes burning into him.

"Go away!" he shouted at his tormentor. Instantly a hard, rough hand closed over his mouth. William struggled to inhale. The iron hand yanked William from his bed.

"Wake the matron up," said the Boy in a whisper, "and I'll kill ye!"

Instinct told William he was no match for this monster. But he had to breathe or die.

The other sleepers did not stir; either frequent nighttime excitement had made them immune to noise, or perhaps they, too, feared for their lives, as William did. Finally the Boy eased his grip on his prey.

"No more crying and keeping me awake, do ye hear?" he hissed, then shook William like a rag doll. The little boy could only nod, swallowing his tears.

The days drifted by in a gray haze. Although the school provided little religious training, William remembered a Scripture he had heard his father read: "I will not be afraid what man can do unto me" (Psalm 56:11). *God will help me!* thought the little boy. Relief and optimism flowed through him—until his next encounter with the Boy!

William learned to say his letters, study his numbers, make his bed, and eat his porridge in silence. Perhaps if he remained in the background, the Boy would not notice him. "I well remember being afraid to lift up my eyes upon him higher than his knees. . . . I knew him by his shoe-buckles better than any other part of his dress," William wrote later.[4]

But the fifteen year old rarely lost an opportunity to torture younger students. William never mentioned his name, even fifty years later. He thought of him as the Boy—a predator that locked him in dank, ancient cellars, held his head under water in rain barrels, and appeared like an evil spirit by his bed at night. For two years, William grew accustomed to living in terror. He did not tell his father about the Boy when he went home for brief holiday visits. He told no one, as William knew the day he did, he would die.

But one day the school grew alive with cautious celebration—the Boy, who tormented many other small children, had been caught in the act! Dr. Pittman, the headmaster, questioned possible victims. He called William in.

"Cowper, has he frightened you in any way, even in jest?" The tall man with the piercing gaze scared William almost as much as the Boy. He would not answer, even if Dr. Pittman used the dreaded cane on him. He must not. . . .

Although Dr. Pittman wore a severe expression, he possessed a genuine concern for his students. The animal fear in William's eyes, mirrored in those of a half dozen other little boys he had interviewed, told the headmaster what he wanted to know. He had the Boy brought to him and, with an efficient and merciless arm, extracted the truth.

"Look! He is leaving, and holidays don't begin for a fortnight!" exclaimed Peter, an older boy in William's dormitory. All the children gathered around the window as they watched their late enemy depart in a coach, his sullen face lowered on his chest. Expelled!

After his first ecstasy at the Boy's downfall, William dreaded his possible return. He had prayed for days his enemy would die. Would God punish William for being so wicked and allow the fiend to return to the next bed?

A severe eye infection endangered his sight, so his father sent him, now age eight, to live with a famous London eye doctor. William resided there until he was ten years old, when he began attending Westminster School. He studied Greek and Latin and found he enjoyed the classics. The schoolboy also began writing poetry for fun, and penned the following ode:

> To rescue from the tyrant's sword
> The oppress'd—unseen and unimplor'd
> To cheer the face of woe;

From lawless insult to defend
An orphan's right—a fallen friend,
And a forgiven foe:

These, these, distinguish from the crowd,
And these alone, the great and good,
The guardians of mankind.
Whose bosoms with these virtues heave!
Oh! With what matchless speed, they leave
The multitude behind! [5]

One evening, as he made his way through the churchyard of St. Margaret's, William saw a light shining among the tombs. A delicious thrill of horror crawled up his spine.

Perhaps it is the spirit of old Mistress Hutchinson, thought William. Memories of the pious old cook, who had died a week before at Westminster, flooded his mind. *Has she not yet gone to heaven?* Curiosity overcame fear, and he crept towards the grave.

His lantern glowing in the purple twilight, a burly grave-digger lofted shovelfuls of dirt. William watched, fascinated—until the man threw a large spadeful in William's direction. Clods and dust rained down on him as he hid behind a tomb. *I'll sneeze! He'll see me!* A smooth, hard object struck his leg; in the lamplight, William saw two dark, round holes and broken, grinning teeth. *A skull!*

William froze like a doomed rabbit, then ran through the shadowy streets back to school as if a demon's long fingers grabbed for his coattails. He lay in bed, shivering uncontrollably and promising God to be good forever. *I will pray as Dr. Nicholls does,* he vowed.

Kind, devout Dr. Nicholls, who schooled William and his classmates in preparation for confirmation, would go to heaven when he died, reasoned William. For two panic-stricken weeks he mimicked his mentor's every move, puzzling but gratifying the good man.

Soon he found constant prayer sessions senseless and boring. *How can Dr. Nicholls stay on his knees so long?* William, kneeling beside his bed after the matron had taken away the candle, felt his own legs ache, his body swaying as he dozed off.

"Will, God does not listen to snores," said his friend Charles, poking William. "Why waste His time and yours?"

Gradually, William's terrors lessened and his prayer times with them. Soon William managed to forget all he learned about God during confirmation classes.

When he celebrated his eighteenth birthday, he left Westminster and lived at home for nine months, the longest period of time he spent there.

"William, it is time you began a profession; you must study the law," said his father. He apprenticed him to a Mr. Chapman for three years. Four societies, housed in inns, existed in London, where British barristers learned and practiced their trade: Inner Temple, Middle Temple, Lincoln Inn, and Grey's Inn. Rev. Cowper enrolled William in the Middle Temple.

The vigorous young man began one of the happiest periods of his life—but not because he enjoyed memorizing the intricate details of British law! William hated every moment of the profession his father had assigned him and avoided study as much as possible. But he and his friend Edward Thurlow, another law clerk who eventually became Lord Chancellor, spent hours at the home of his uncle Ashley Cowper in Southampton Row. His daughters Theodora and Harriet, both lovely and lively, made their visits a joy. Later he reminded Harriet, then Lady Hesketh, of the days when the young men were "constantly employed from morning till night in giggling and making giggle, instead of studying the law."[6]

When teasing the girls did not occupy William, he whiled away his time with other members of the Nonsense Club. He and his friends—Charles Churchill, Bonnell Thornton, George Colman, and Robert Lloyd—founded the group, which conducted meetings at local pubs where they ate and drank, joked and debated the merits of the barmaids. William, although not as flamboyant as some of his friends, captivated them with his storytelling. But the Nonsense Club also conducted passionate political, literary, and theatrical debates, arguing late into the night. They composed poetry which parodied English society. They studied literature and created their own periodicals and wrote for others.

Such a life intoxicated the young student. *I had no idea, when I was attending those miserable schools as a boy, how good it is to learn with those of like mind!*

None of this advanced his law career, but Mr. Chapman rarely interfered with William's self-directed literary and political education. Rev. Cowper tolerated his lack of interest in his studies. Perhaps William would one day mature and concentrate better.

But William's uncle Ashley Cowper grew concerned as he observed the increasing interest William showed in his daughter Theodora. Ashley had enjoyed William's company as much as his girls and had not worried about possible attachments, as William spent just as much time with Harriet as Theodora! But more and more, Ashley had noted his Theodora's attraction to the strongly built, blond young man with the charismatic smile. Now he scowled as his daughter, her face aglow with love, clasped William's hands as he was leaving.

"Will you come for Christmas dinner, William?" asked the young woman, her eyes dancing with anticipation.

He melted under her inviting smile.

"Father would *so* like you to join us," she insisted.

"Of course, I shall come," said William tenderly. He did not notice Ashley Cowper had *not* echoed the invitation. William idealized Theodora as "Delia" in love poems and visualized a life in which they would spend every moment together.

He clung to his carefree lifestyle throughout his twenties. William especially loved going to the theater and opera houses with the Nonsense Club. But even their camaraderie could not dispel the gloom and restlessness that began to haunt his nights.

"Didn't you sleep, old chap?" asked his friend Thornton one

morning, observing William's haggard eyes and pale face.

"Not much. Penelope and her brood keep me awake with their scampering and scrabbling." Although William was exhausted, he still smiled at the thought of the mouse and her six babies he had befriended in his chambers at the Middle Temple.

"I'll loan you my cat; old Tinker will make short work of the whole lot."

"So, as in all the world, an execution of the innocent is the only answer for peace."

Thornton drank his tea and said nothing. Lately pessimistic remarks had chained William's conversations, weighing them down with misery. He and other Nonsense Club members noted his depression with concern but could not ascertain how to lift it.

William gulped his own tea, grimacing. "Today I suppose I must go view a trial at the Temple."

"We all must, sooner or later, old man," said his friend, trying to assume a jovial tone. "After all, we are here to study The Law." He made a deep, mocking bow.

William shrugged, his face limp and hopeless. "Is that why I exist—to squander my days on trivialities until I die?" He rose without another word and plodded down the street, his head low on his chest.

The night after their encounter, Thornton met William and other Nonsense Club members at an alehouse. William was at his best—bright, witty, humorous. Thornton watched his hazel eyes glint as William drank a very proper but sarcastic toast to the king, his smiling rhetoric entrancing those at the tables around them.

Good to see him smile, thought Thornton. *But he smiles too much; he laughs as if he has drunk many tankards of ale, and I know he has emptied only one. He embraces everyone who will give him an ear, stranger or friend. That is not like him.*

For a year, Thornton and William's other friends watched him descend into the blackest of moods for weeks at a time, with brief periods of irrational celebration. His gloom darkened when his father died in 1856. Despite their distant relationship, Rev.

Cowper's death devastated his son. Later William remembered this first major brush with the depression that was to cloud his life: "I was struck. . .with such a dejection of spirits, as none but they who have felt the same can have the least conception of. Day and night I was upon the rack, lying down in horror, rising up in despair."[7] Some would later connect William's depression with religion, but at this period of his life, William cherished few, if any, religious convictions.

During these painful days, William continued to see Theodora whenever he could summon enough energy. She listened to him for hours, comforting and encouraging him.

My malady does not seem to lessen her love for me. William became more convinced than ever Theodora was the woman for him.

But Ashley Cowper finally stepped between them.

"William, I have loved you as a son, but marriage between you and Theodora cannot happen."

William stared at his uncle, uncomprehending.

"It *must not be,*" said Ashley. "Unlike some, I do not approve of marriages between close relatives. Too, we have fallen on difficult times; I possess only a small dowry for my daughter."

William's very breath strangled him. He could not think. *I must speak. Move, tongue! Mouth, open!* "I do not require a large dowry, Uncle," he said at last.

"How shall you care for Theodora? You are twenty-six years old; you studied law for seven years and even passed the bar two years ago. But I have seen no indication you intend to practice law."

William swallowed hard. "I shall take my profession more seriously, sir, in the future."

Ashley sighed. "I have no doubt you harbor the best of intentions—"

"My father left me an inheritance."

"Your father," said Ashley, "was a good man, but he could not possibly have left you enough to support a wife and family."

William stared at his scuffed old shoes. "If I prove my love

124

by hard work and dedication this year to come, may I hope for your consent, sir, to our marriage? For Theodora loves me, and I her." He could not keep a quiver from his voice.

"No." Ashley rose. "I do not forbid you to visit us, William; I have ever loved you and love you still. But I do ask you to avoid my daughter. I shall not allow her to see you. William, do not speak to Theodora if you should meet, do not write her, nor approach her in any way. If you love her, as you say, you will not interfere with her future happiness."

Ashley watched the young man leave through the front gate, the pouring rain filling his hat brim, overflowing to soak his bowed shoulders and his pinched gray face as he took one last look at the window of his beloved's room. A deluge of regret filled the father's heart. *I should have halted the love affair long ago. But they had such merry times together, the cousins! I had hoped Theodora or Harriet would fall in love with William's friend, Edward Thurlow! Despite his youthful foolishness, Thurlow will no doubt achieve a brilliant future. I did right in forbidding the match between William and Theodora; I must think no more about it. He is unstable and harbors gloomy, angry notions—not the man to make my sweet Theodora happy. She is young; she will forget William and find another.*

About the same time he lost Theodora, William's young friend, Sir William Russel, drowned in the Thames River.

How can I live? grieved William. *My love, snatched from me as if I were evil incarnate, and my best friend, cold and lifeless as this miserable day.*

He expressed his suffering in a sad poem:

Still, still, I mourn with each returning day,
Him snatch'd by fate in early youth away;
And her—through tedious years of doubt and pain
Fix'd in her choice and faithful—but in vain![8]

Neither William nor Theodora married. Although she, through relatives, made secret contributions to his income throughout his life, William would never see her again. He did not mention her in any of his writings, not even in his later extensive correspondence with her sister, Harriet.

two

William now lived at the Inner Temple and finally obtained the post of bankruptcy commissioner, which earned him sixty pounds a year. Although a meager salary, he welcomed every penny. William, carefree and generous to his friends, had spent his inheritance. He continued to invest most of his time and energy in the literary activities of the Nonsense Club. When, at thirty-one, he was recommended for a higher administrative position in the House of Lords, William and his friends celebrated his success.

"Perhaps my fortunes are changing," he told the Nonsense Club.

But it was not to be. Party controversies delayed William's job. In the end, those in power agreed to grant him the clerkship, on one condition: William must qualify by passing an examination before the House of Lords.

"You can do it!"

"We know you will pass with flying colors!"

"No one could do better than you, Will!"

His friends all encouraged him. For the first time in his legal career, William reviewed and studied with all his might in preparation for the dreaded test—to no avail. Upon this failure, William sequestered himself and refused to see his friends. He could not sleep for days. When he did, he dreamed of standing before the House of Lords in blank, idiotic silence. Wolfish anxiety ripped him with fangs of fear. A descent into madness seemed the only answer. William's mind spiraled down, down into the deepest depression. He tried to pray but soon abandoned his efforts. He felt God Himself hated him and sought to destroy him forever. In the midst of his agony, William wrote despairing lines:

> *Hatred and vengeance,—my eternal portion,*
> *Scarce can endure delay of execution,—*
> *Wait, with impatient readiness to seize my*
> *Soul in a moment.*
>
> *Damned below Judas: more abhorred than he was,*
> *Who for a few pence sold his Holy Master!*
> *Twice betrayed Jesus me, the last delinquent,*
> *Deems the profanest.*
>
> *Man disavows, and Deity disowns me;*
> *Hell might afford my miseries a shelter;*
> *Therefore, Hell keeps her ever-hungry mouths all*
> *Bolted against me.*[1]

William tried to kill himself, first with an overdose of laudanum, an opium-based painkiller, then with a dagger. When friends found him in his room, hanging by his stocking garters, they took him to his brother John, now twenty-six years old and a Fellow at Corpus Christi College.

William, wild-eyed and shivering, cried, "Oh, brother, I am lost! Think of eternity, and then think what it is to be lost!"[2]

John, overwhelmed at his agony, embraced him. His brother's kindness calmed the distraught William, and he slept for three hours. But when he awoke, the madness he had so desired possessed him—he screamed with pain, holding his head. "If it were possible that a heavy blow could light on the brain, without touching the skull, such was the sensation I felt. . . . At every stroke my thoughts and expressions became more wild and incoherent; all that remained clear was the sense of sin, and the expectation of punishment."[3]

John consulted Dr. Nathaniel Cotton, who ran an asylum in St. Albans. "Is there any hope for my poor brother?" asked John, his eyes full of misery.

"With Christ," answered the doctor gently, "there is always hope." Dr. Cotton welcomed the raving William to his asylum, calming him as best he could with doses of laudanum. Laudanum, which induced sleep, was prescribed for most mental illnesses in the 1700s, but it also sometimes aggravated symptoms such as nightmares and hallucinations. Days of treatment brought William no return to sanity, but very gradually, his days grew less painful and more rational. Dr. Cotton began to introduce Christian truths to William, who had absorbed elementary knowledge of religion throughout his school days but possessed only a dread of God.

"William, did you know Jesus Christ has paid every debt you owe?" asked Dr. Cotton one day as they sat together at tea.

"I hope He is of immense fortune," answered William, with a ghost of a smile, "as I imagine my tailor still seeks me for the enormous sum I owe him, as do the grocers and candle makers."

His host gave a quiet chuckle, then declared, "I think you know of what we truly speak."

William's smile disappeared; his haunted face grew bleak as the fall afternoon. "There is no relief for my sin. God wants nothing to do with me, Dr. Cotton."

"Indeed? How can that be, when His holy Word decrees otherwise?" Dr. Cotton opened his worn Bible and read, " 'Being justified freely by his grace through the redemption that is in Christ Jesus: Whom God hath set forth to be a propitiation through faith in his blood, to declare his righteousness for the remission of sins that are past, through the forbearance of God' (Romans 3:24–25). Jesus Christ paid for your sins with His blood, William; you are free from them. As a man in debtor's prison is set free through his friend's payment of his debts, so are you set free from all your sins, through the generosity of Christ."

"Please, may I read that?" William stared at the Bible and pondered, "Why would He do such a thing?"

"I have no idea—except that He must love you with all His heart," answered Dr. Cotton. He said no more but prayed in silence, as he had for days, for his obsessive, brilliant patient.

William read in the Bible about Jesus and Lazarus; Jesus' love and grief for His dead friend moved him deeply. He read the fifth chapter of Romans himself, then again, and again.

"Immediately I received strength to believe it, and the full beams of the Sun of Righteousness shone upon me. I saw the sufficiency of the atonement he had made, my pardon sealed in his blood, and all the fulness [sic] and completeness of his justification. In a moment I believed, and received the gospel."[4]

Now when I awake each morning, I do not wish myself dead. God smiles at me, and I return the smile. Every day William thanked God he had not destroyed himself.

Exultant, John reported to Dr. Cotton after a visit, "William is like his old self—no, better! He laughs; he rejoices! He welcomes God as a friend, not an enemy who desires his end." The young minister embraced the physician in gratitude. "I shall arrange a home for him near me."

"William is yet fragile," cautioned Dr. Cotton. His patient's abrupt mood change worried him. Although physicians would not coin the term "bipolar disorder" until much later, the eighteenth-century doctor recognized patterns of the disease in his friend. "Permit William to remain here at St. Albans for a time, then I shall release him to your care."

John agreed, and William stayed at the asylum almost two years, until 1765. As he recovered, William studied the Scriptures and spent many pleasant hours talking with Dr. Cotton, who enjoyed their stimulating conversations. Poetry began to flow from his pen, rich songs of joy and thanksgiving, including the hymn "The Happy Change," which was later published in the Olney collection:

How blest thy creature is, O God,
    When, with a single eye,
He views the luster of thy word,
    The day-spring from on high!

Through all the storms that veil the skies,
    And frown on earthly things,
The Sun of Righteousness he eyes,
    With healing in his wings.

Struck by that light, the human heart,
    A barren soil no more,
Sends the sweet smell of grace abroad,
    Where serpents lurk'd before.[5]

To his cousin Harriet, who had married and now was known as Lady Hesketh, he described himself as "a convert made in Bedlam."[6] He wrote of God's work during his miserable depression: "Terrible as this chastisement is, I acknowledge in it the hand of an infinite justice; nor is it at all more difficult for me to perceive in it the hand of an infinite mercy likewise: When I consider the effect it has had upon me, I am exceedingly thankful for it, and without hypocrisy, esteem it the greatest blessing, next to life itself, I ever received from the divine bounty. I pray God that I may ever retain this sense of it, and then I am sure I shall continue to be, as I am at present, really happy."[7]

Every day God sends me a hundred messages of His goodness. William greeted each morning with gladness. Warm friendships, the fragrance of hot bread, glorious sunshine, delicate flowers, even rainy days brought him intense joy after a long, dark period of despair. He wrote later, "I never received a *little* pleasure from any thing in my life; if I am delighted, it is in the extreme."[8]

When William left the asylum in 1765, John helped find a house in Huntingdon, Cambridge, about fifteen miles from his own home. They saw each other often and enjoyed writing and translating poetry together, even coauthoring a magazine article.

William had resigned from his job as bankruptcy commissioner and now depended on his brother and other relatives for financial support. Despite his improved mental condition, William still managed money poorly; he spent a year's income within three months. Nor did he cope well living with only a servant. Despondency descended upon him in the periods between his brother's visits. John knew he needed more socialization and daily care.

William, without intention, solved the problem himself.

One Sunday after church, he struck up a conversation with an undergraduate student named William Unwin. Young Unwin invited him home for tea, and William met his family: his father Morley, a well-educated former pastor who tutored students in classical literature; mother Mary, a kind woman who loved to read; and sister Susanna, a shy but pleasant teenager. Devout, intellectual Methodists, sociable but not fashionable, the Unwins made William feel at home.

"Mr. Cowper, do have more scones," urged Mrs. Unwin. "You should eat more, you know. Your mother must certainly desire your health and well-being!"

William gave a sad smile. "Perhaps—my mother is in heaven."

His hostess gazed at him with compassion. "You may be sure she desires it," was all she said, but her gentle eyes and motherly smile warmed William inside even more than the steaming cup of tea she poured for him.

Within a few weeks, the Unwins had welcomed William as a boarder, despite his near-bankruptcy. For the rest of his life, he would live as a cherished, though often troubled, member of their household. He regarded the son, William, as one of his best friends. Mrs. Mary Unwin, though only seven years older than himself, became a substitute mother. William flourished in the simple, structured atmosphere. Every day, the Unwins breakfasted at eight, then read Scriptures or sermons until eleven o'clock, when the family went to church. William spent the next few hours reading and writing, including long letters to his cousin

Harriet Hesketh. He also loved riding or gardening, which he found therapeutic throughout his life. He referred to himself as a "great florist and shrub-doctor."[9] The family gathered in the garden during fine weather for theological discussions until tea-time, then took walks of three or four miles. After dinner, they sang hymns as Mrs. Unwin played the harpsichord, or they all discussed the latest sermon. William and the Unwins prayed together, then went to bed.

That such a family should welcome me as their own! Thanks be to You, Lord!

William considered becoming a clergyman but did not sense God's call, as he doubted his ability to communicate before large groups. *But I do enjoy conversing with my friends, and we write often; perhaps I can speak the gospel to individuals more effectively than before great crowds, as John Wesley and George Whitefield do.*

William described Huntingdon as flat and uninteresting, with few trees. In winter, floods turned it into icy swampland. Yet contentment, like a warm blanket, surrounded him as he gave thanks for his newfound peace with God: "Once he was a terror to me, and his service, O what a weariness it was! Now I can say, I love him and his holy name, and am never so happy as when I speak of his mercies to me."[10]

three

"M istress Unwin! Come quickly!"

"Why, Harry, what is wrong?" Mary, who had just tied her Sunday bonnet ribbons, stared at the young farmer.

"It's Rev. Unwin, mum. His horse has thrown 'im! 'E's in a bad way at my house. Be pleased to hurry, mum!"

In a daze, William and the family rode to Harry's cottage. *Rev. Unwin? Surely not!* thought William. *I heard him only this morning, whistling as he rode early to pray at the church!*

When they arrived, Mary threw herself down at her husband's side, sobbing. Rev. Unwin lay in a coma, groaning on the rude bed, his head covered with bloody bandages. Their son hovered close, clasping his mother and sister with trembling arms. Although shaken, William tried to comfort them as best he could. They could not move the injured man, so the Unwins remained by his side. During the next few days, their patient occasionally gained consciousness. Although his speech was slurred, those around him knew he was praying.

Four days after the accident in July 1767, Rev. Morley Unwin died.

"What shall we do? Where shall we go?" wept Mary after the funeral. "I cannot remain here, where my dear husband and

I spent so many pleasant hours together!"

"I do not know, dear lady," said William, choking with grief.

He and the Unwins sank into a pit of despondency. *We all quake, as if the earth beneath us may give way any moment*, thought William. Nightmares about death had begun to trouble him again; his head ached without ceasing, as if the pain in his heart had infected it.

One afternoon William returned from a solitary horseback ride to greet a stranger in the Unwins' parlor. "Good day, sir."

"God be with you," answered the stocky man with the penetrating eyes.

William Unwin said, "You know I have mentioned Mr. John Newton, my new friend. He is the curate at Olney, but traveled here at the request of Dr. Conyers, who knows of our tragedy."

"Thanks be to God for your good comfort, sir," said Mary. William noted her cheeks grew a little less pale, her eyes brighter as Newton read Scriptures and prayed with her.

Was this man really a slave trader? wondered William as he listened to the plain but powerful pastor expound upon the Bible. Young Unwin had told him of Newton's background and radical conversion to Christ. William hated the slave trade. He could hardly reconcile the kind, profoundly spiritual man before him with someone who kidnapped bewildered people from their native land, stuffing ships with men, women, and little children as if they were animals to be sold. Hundreds of Africans died of disease, thirst, and malnutrition on these sea voyages. Brutal overseers beat and tortured them if they defended their wives or children. William's stomach lurched with repulsion. He spoke before he thought.

"Surely, sir, such an occupation never touched you!"

"Oh, but it did," answered John Newton. "Not only touched, but consumed me—and for what? For filthy monetary gain! I have seen the dying faces of slaves in my dreams for many a year." He paused, then stared directly into William's eyes. "No man bore blacker sin than mine. Yet the Savior forgave me."

William closed his eyes; joy overflowed in warm tears down

his cheeks. *To feel clean, unspotted as Mary's laundry dancing in the sunny June breezes!* "The Savior has forgiven me, too," he said simply.

"Then we rejoice together!" Newton beamed and clasped William's hand in his strong grasp, then turned to Mary Unwin. "Of course, you must come to Olney," he said. "Orchard Side, a house near my own, is empty. My good wife and I should be glad to help you secure this residence and become our neighbors. Our church would welcome you as family."

William and the Unwins exchanged glances. *Has God sent us His ministering angel so soon?* thought William.

"We shall certainly consider your kind offer, Mr. Newton," said Mary.

After he left, all felt refreshed, as if a cool, bubbling stream were rinsing away their troubles. William later wrote Newton: "Most of your other connexions [*sic*] you may fairly be said to have formed by your own act; but your connexion with me was the work of God."[1]

Within a few months, William and the Unwin family found themselves in Olney, a town of two thousand poverty-stricken inhabitants, most of them lace makers who worked ten to twelve hours a day creating their delicate merchandise. William wrote, "Olney is a populous place, inhabited chiefly by the half-starved and the ragged of the Earth."[2] Because their parents worked long, exhausting hours, neglected children wandered in the streets, fighting, vandalizing, and stealing whenever possible.

But John Newton saw opportunity for these families' salvation and healing. His patron, John Thornton, provided two hundred pounds each year to purchase food and clothing for the poor. He involved William, who became a kind of lay pastor, in his work.

"Squire Cowper comes! The Squire is here!" Hungry little ones in Olney greeted William with hugs as he brought their families bread, candles, and blankets to warm them in their miserable huts. He prayed with their grateful parents and read Scriptures with them. William found himself happier as he visited the needy and comforted the sick and dying in the name of Christ. Later John Newton would write he never saw a man more dedicated to loving and serving others than William Cowper.

William also became interested in carpentry. "There is not a squire in all the country," he wrote, "who can boast of having made better squirrel-houses, hutches for rabbits, or bird-cages, than myself." He created "tables, such as they were, and joint-stools, such as never were."[3] William, who had once thought only to destroy his own life, now wanted to build. He also began drawing landscapes when his eyesight did not trouble him, celebrating the natural beauty around him with his pencils and charcoals.

William and the Unwins loved Orchard Side, their new abode. William cared for the garden, planting traditional flowers and vegetables, as well as trial plots of melons, cucumbers, and pineapples. Only a small apothecary's herb garden separated Orchard Side's garden from John Newton's. When the two families found themselves visiting every day, they offered Thomas Aspray, the herb garden's owner, a guinea per year to allow them to walk on his land.

"My wife and I grieve with you in the sad loss of Rev. Unwin," said Newton, clasping his neighbors' hands as they prayed together. "But we cherish you more each day."

As we do you, Rev. Newton. William had felt his own depression lighten somewhat, his headaches lessen in intensity. *In your kindness, the Unwins and I have found a true refuge.*

Aspray also allowed William to write in his little summerhouse, originally built in the apothecary's garden to house smokers, as smoking was not permitted indoors during the 1700s. William sometimes called it his "verse manufactory."[4] The summerhouse proved an ideal retreat: "I write in a nook that I call my *boudoir;* it is a summer-house not much bigger than a sedan chair, the door of which opens into the garden that is now crowded with pinks, roses and honeysuckles and the window into my neighbour's orchard."[5] William wrote poetry and letters by the hundreds, sitting in the tiny house. He rarely traveled, so his witty correspondence kept him in touch with his host of devoted friends and relatives. Future literary critics would regard his letters as equal or surpassing his poetry.

Despite his struggles with depression, William's transparent, often childlike charm endeared him to many. He had carried on a correspondence with his cousin Harriet Hesketh for years, but now he wrote her constantly. William spoke of great affection for Harriet, which sometimes bordered on adoration, but did not hold the romantic passion he had experienced for her sister, Theodora: "Adieu, my dear Cousin! so much as I love you, I wonder how it has happened I was never in love with you. Thank Heaven that I never was, for at this time I have had a pleasure in writing to you, which, in that case, I should have forfeited. Let me hear from you, or I shall reap but half the reward that is due to my noble indifference."[6]

When Mary Unwin suffered a serious illness in 1769, a distraught William helped care for her and prayed desperately for her recovery. *But no matter how much I love Mary, God reigns in my affections. He must have first place in my heart.* William wrote a hymn, "Walking with God," its later title taken from the opening line:

> *O for a closer walk with God,*
> *   A calm and heavenly frame;*
> *A light to shine upon the road*
> *   That leads me to the Lamb!*

> *The dearest idol I have known,*
> *   Whate'er that idol be,*
> *Help me to tear it from Thy throne,*
> *   And worship only Thee.*

> *So shall my walk be close with God,*
> *   Calm and serene my frame:*
> *So purer light shall mark the road*
> *   That leads me to the Lamb.*[7]

When Mary recovered, William's relief knew no bounds.

John Newton was a frequent summerhouse visitor. The two prayed together and discussed the texts of Newton's sermons for hours on flower-fragrant, drowsy summer afternoons.

How blest I am to have a friend like this! thought William. *He is a true brother in Christ, the older brother I never had.*

When Newton's prayer meetings outgrew the church and were relocated in the local Great House, William, thinking of their close friendship, wrote "On Opening a Place for Social Prayer," which was sung at the first meeting there:

> *Jesus! Where'er thy people meet,*
> *There they behold thy mercy-seat;*
> *Where'er they seek thee, thou art found,*
> *And every place is hallow'd ground.*[8]

Their continued relationship generated more deep conversations, more spiritual insights, and more hymns written by William. He missed William Unwin, who had become a pastor himself and moved away, but he wrote him constantly. He grieved over his brother John's early death in 1770, but his close friendship with Newton gave him the courage to collaborate in writing a collection of hymns to sing in church. Many Anglican church authorities accepted only the singing of Scripture; they rejected hymns as radical and unspiritual.

"We praise God with the singing of psalms, and that is good," said John Newton. "But God is doing a new thing amongst us!"

"We must sing a new song to Him!" agreed William. "A song of His love and His forgiveness!" During 1772–1773 he would write sixty-seven of the 348 Olney hymns, including "There Is a Fountain," originally entitled "Peace for the Fountain Opened." William wrote this still-popular hymn after meditating upon Zechariah 13:1, "In that day there shall be a fountain opened to the house of David and to the inhabitants of Jerusalem for sin and for uncleanness."

> *There is a fountain fill'd with blood*
> > *Drawn from Emmanuel's veins,*
> *And sinners plunged beneath that flood*
> > *Lose all their guilty stains.*

> *The dying thief rejoiced to see*
> > *That fountain in his day,*
> *And there have I, though vile as he,*
> > *Wash'd all my sins away.*[9]

"Is not the love of God grand," asked Newton softly, "that he should forgive such as I?" The former slave trader began to write:

> *Amazing grace! how sweet the sound*
> *That saved a wretch like me!*
> *I once was lost, but now am found,*
> *Was blind, but now I see.*[10]

"God's love is magnificent, indeed," answered William. His heart swelled with gratitude and worship as he read his friend's hymn. He wrote:

> *'Tis joy enough, my All in All,*
> > *At thy dear feet to lie;*
> *Thou wilt not let me lower fall*
> > *And none can higher fly.*[11]

The more William studied the Bible with John Newton, the more he wanted to praise God for communicating His thoughts to man. William wrote "The Light and Glory of the Word," another Olney hymn, to describe his reverence for the Scriptures:

> *The Spirit breathes upon the Word,*
> > *And brings the truth to sight;*
> *Precepts and promises afford*
> > *A sanctifying light.*

A glory gilds the sacred page,
*   Majestic like the sun;*
It gives a light to every age,
*   It gives, but borrows none.*

The hand that gave it still supplies
*   The gracious light and heat:*
His truths upon the nations rise,
*   They rise, but never set.*[12]

John Newton intended the hymn collection to be a joint affair. But William, who had battled despondency with his brother John's death, began to sink into another deep depression. *John lives, whole and rejoicing in God's presence. But my sad, injured heart languishes here on earth!* William felt the all-too-familiar black clouds of despair boiling within him; in another Olney hymn, he prayed:

Heal us, Emmanuel, here we are,
*   Waiting to feel thy touch:*
Deep-wounded souls to thee repair,
*   And Saviour, we are such.*

Our faith is feeble, we confess,
*   We faintly trust thy word:*
But wilt thou pity us the less?
*   Be that far from thee, Lord!*

Remember him who once applied,
*   With trembling for relief;*
"Lord, I believe," with tears he cried,
*   "Oh, help my unbelief!"*[13]

William's instability grew when Susanna Unwin married Rev. Matthew Powley in 1772 and moved away. Whispers about her mother and William began to circulate.

" 'Tisn't decent, for a man to bide alone with a woman."

"He *says* she be a mother to him. A mother? Or perhaps a wife!"

"Now, now, I've no doubt they are fond of each other. Mary and William should marry as soon as possible. It's the only proper thing to do."

Relatives, uneasy about the family's reputation, began to insist on the marriage.

William felt the walls of social convention pressing on every side. *Why do even our godly friends listen to stupid rumors? Why do they believe the worst of us, when we have done nothing to deserve it?*

Finally, William and Mary announced their engagement, and all Olney gave an approving nod.

But William's mental state deteriorated into total despair.

One night, after wandering the house like a tortured phantom, he dropped into a fitful sleep. A deep, hollow voice, like the hollow striking of a clock in the darkness, awoke him. Hot sweat poured from his fevered body. William grasped the bedclothes as if he had claws.

"William Cowper," the voice intoned.

Who? . . . Where? . . . William could not think. He could not see. He lay motionless, weighed down with lead-heavy evil. He gasped for breath, but the demon darkness smothered his parched mouth, as if with sand.

"William Cowper," said the voice, then spoke in Latin: *"Actum est de te, periiste! Periiste!"* [14]

It is over with me? William cringed in terror, like a mouse paralyzed in the face of a giant predator's teeth. *I must perish forever? Eternally? O, God. . .O, God! Why do You desert me? Why have You forsaken me?*

Hellish flames leaped from the very walls. Agony cut through his brain like a sword, and William felt himself falling down, down into nothingness.

four

Several years would pass before this episode of depression subsided. His nightmares tortured him. He again tried to kill himself, believing he should sacrifice himself to God, as Abraham was to offer Isaac. He accused Mary Unwin of poisoning him. He avoided meat, insisting it was human tissue. When he arrived at John Newton's home and refused to leave, the minister took William in, where once again he slowly recovered under the care of Dr. Nathaniel Cotton and the fervent prayers of his friends. In May 1774 he returned to live at Orchard Side with Mary.

"You will take me home with you?" asked William, like a child.

Mary's doelike eyes shone with compassion in her weary face. "Of course." Her solicitude had not abated, despite William's earlier wild allegations. In order to care for William, she, too, had taken temporary residence with the Newtons.

This time, when the two began living alone, no one harassed them about marriage.

But the delusion that God had deserted him did not dissipate. William never did resume church attendance, and he rarely prayed, believing God preferred no contact with him.

William avoided talking to anyone but Mary, his doctor, and the Newtons. But he domesticated three rabbits given him by neighbors whose children had tired of them. Since the days he nurtured Penelope the mouse and her brood while living in the Middle Temple, William had loved animals. Now the soft fur, placid eyes, and wiggling noses of the hares soothed his anxiety. He named them Tiney, Puss, and Bess. William built cages that he kept in a side hallway, but he often allowed them to run free in the hall and brought them into the parlor, where Bess, the largest, intimidated the cat. Later he would immortalize his pets in *The Task*, a series of long poems.

One August day, Puss chewed through the lattice door he had installed so his animals might have air.

"Squire Cowper, 'as one o' your 'ares gotten out?" Young Charlie, who lived down the road, called to William from the front door.

William dropped the book he had been reading and scrambled into the hallway. "Puss! She's escaped!" He ran outside, his heart pounding. Charlie ran after the swift little animal, his skinny legs bounding down the dusty road.

Silly, adventurous Puss—the village abounded with dogs! Was she fast enough to evade their sharp teeth?

William's friend Thomas Freeman met him at the door and said, "I tried to throw my hat over her, but she ran like the devil himself was chasing her!" They both took off, as Richard Coleman, another friend, joined them in the pursuit.

William soon slowed, gasping. Now middle-aged, he was no match for Puss's speed. Thomas became the next dropout in the race. But Richard pursued her with determination—through a crowd of village people and dogs!

"Hold your dogs!" Richard shouted to the group. Some obliged and grabbed their animals as they leaped and growled. Half the village population chased the terrified rabbit in a mad race toward the edge of town.

William's sides heaved. If only he could run as he did when a boy! *What will happen to Puss? Will I ever see her again?* He shuddered as the dogs tried to yank away from their masters.

"She be goin' to the tanner's!" yelled Charlie. Even the teenager looked winded.

But Richard outdistanced the pack of pursuers; he pelted into the tanner's yard in time to see one of the workmen pull a wet, wriggling Puss by her ears from a large water pit used in the process of leathermaking.

"Like to drowned, she did," said the man, grinning. "Fell into one pit, climbed out, then fell into another." He handed the rabbit to Richard. "But Sunday dinner didn't get away!"

"Much obliged," said Richard, who rinsed lime from the tanning pits from Puss's fur and threw her into a burlap sack, shouldering it as he walked toward Orchard Side. *William is a perfect fool about his animals; if I had not captured Puss, he would have lain awake every night worrying about her. But I am glad the hare is safe. It would have thrown William into another attack of despondency if those dogs had torn Puss to pieces.* As he trudged into sight, William's ecstatic grin repaid him for his dusty, exhausting race.

"Silly Puss!" said William as he stroked the tired animal with a tender hand and gave her fresh water. "Do you run from me, who loves you? Or in the name of freedom, do you run from God to those who would devour you? And which is the worst fate?"

Richard shook his head. Even in petting rabbits, William could not forget his gloomy theology.

William wrote a long letter to John Newton in 1780 about Puss's escapade, as his friend had moved to London the year before to assume a pastorate there. In his letters, William shared his moments of light, as well as his darkest feelings with his old friend: "[My thoughts] turn, too, upon spiritual subjects, but the tallest fellow, and the loudest amongst them all, is he who is continually crying, with a loud voice, *Actum est de te, periiste!* [It is all over with thee. Thou hast perished!]"[1]

But William often combined excruciating passages about his own eternal hopelessness with wit and humor. He wrote Newton about poetry and politics, riddles, and the slave trade. Sometimes he wrote an entire letter in humorous verse: "My very dear Friend, I am going to send, what when you have read, you may scratch your head, and say, I suppose, there's nobody knows, whether what I have got be verse or not; by the tune and the time, it ought to be rhyme, but if it be, did you ever see, of late or of yore, such a ditty before?"[2]

Once William wrote Newton a poem decrying the high price of fish and French/Dutch dominance of the seas:

Cocoa-nut naught,
Fish too dear,
None must be bought
For us that are here;

No lobster on earth,
That ever I saw,
To me would be worth
Sixpence a claw.

So, dear Madam, wait
Till fish can be got
At a reas'nable rate
Whether lobster or not;

Till the French and the Dutch
Have quitted the seas,
And then send as much
And as oft as you please.[3]

He frequently wrote William Unwin fond descriptions of his mother, as well as his publishing headaches and scathing denunciations of the government for taxing the poor lace makers' candles. William often sprinkled his letters with humor: "A neighbor of mine in Silver-end keeps an ass; the ass lives on the other side of the garden-wall, and I am writing in the greenhouse. It happens that he is this morning most musically disposed, whether cheered by the fine weather, or some new tune which he has just acquired, or by finding his voice more harmonious than usual. It would be cruel to mortify so fine a singer, therefore I do not tell him that he interrupts and hinders me; but I venture to tell you so, and to plead his performance in excuse for my abrupt conclusion."[4]

He treasured his friends and craved letters from them. Once he needled Joseph Hill, a friend from Nonsense Club days, for his gift of a fine cod but lack of a written reply: "I write, and you send me a fish. This is very well, but not altogether what I want. I wish to hear from you, because the fish, though he serves to convince me that you have me still in remembrance, says not a word of those that sent him, and with respect to your and Mrs. Hill's health, prosperity and happiness, leaves me as much in the dark as before."[5]

Cold weather profoundly impacted William's moods. But even when he discussed it in his letters, he made his remarks sprightly and original, though pessimistic: "Our severest winter, commonly called the spring, is now over. . . ."[6]

Although William missed John Newton and William Unwin, new friends brightened his often miserable days. William Bull, an intelligent, humorous Dissenter, came to his summerhouse to smoke his pipe and banter or talk theology with him. As his friend Newton had hoped, Bull counseled and prayed with William, trying to reassure him of his salvation. Lady Anne Austen, a vivacious, clever widow, rented part of John Newton's former home. Their theological and literary conversations fascinated William. It was Lady Austen's story about the runaway John Gilpin that cheered him during one of his dark moods and inspired the fifty-year-old unknown poet to write the ballad that put his name on the lips of Englishmen everywhere.

Later William wrote William Unwin that he considered his own abilities somewhat mediocre: "I have no more right to the name of a poet than a maker of mouse-traps has to that of an engineer; but my little exploits in this way have at times amused me so much, that I have often wished myself a good one. Such a talent in verse as mine is like a child's rattle;—very entertaining to the trifler that uses it, and very disagreeable to all besides."[7]

The success of "John Gilpin" astonished him. He told

William Unwin that writing humorous poetry helped him cope with the depression that harassed him daily: "Strange as it may seem, the most ludicrous lines I ever wrote have been written in the saddest mood, and, but for that saddest mood, perhaps had never been written at all."[8]

Lady Austen also urged William to write blank verse, one of her favorite genres.

"How can I think of a theme for such a work?" asked William.

"Oh, you can never be in want of a subject—you can write upon any; write upon this sofa," answered the indomitable woman.[9]

William laughed, dipped his pen, and began to write:

I sing the Sofa. I who lately sang
Truth, Hope, and Charity....[10]

His half-serious initial effort grew into *The Task*, a series of long poems, which included "The Sofa," "The Time-Piece," "The Garden," "The Winter Evening," "The Winter Morning Walk," and "The Winter Walk at Noon."

In "The Garden," William painted an extraordinary portrait of his own wounded personality, and God's compassion toward him:

I was a stricken deer, that left the herd
Long since, with many an arrow deep infix'd
My panting side was charged, when I withdrew,
To seek a tranquil death in distant shades.
There was I found by One who had himself
Been hurt by the archers. In his side he bore,
And in his hands and feet the cruel scars.
With gentle force soliciting the darts,
He drew them forth, and heal'd and bade me live.[11]

Despite his continued battles with depression, William celebrated the freedom of his faith in Christ in "The Winter

Morning Walk," another book of *The Task*:

> *Liberty, like day*
> *Breaks on the soul, and by a flash from heaven*
> *Fires all the faculties with glorious joy.*
> *A voice is heard that mortal ears hear not,*
> *Till thou hast touch'd them; 'tis the voice of song,*
> *A loud Hosanna sent from all thy works;*
>
> *Thou art the source and centre of all minds,*
> *Their only point of rest, eternal Word!*[12]

The Task assured William of a prominent place in English literature. For ten years, Britishers read his poetry more than any other author's. While William's writing produced some income, he continued to depend on relatives for support.

His friendship with Lady Austen flourished for three years, then faltered.

"Is she coming yet again today?" asked Mary Unwin.

At her tone, William looked up from his book. "Lady Austen asks me to critique a poem she wrote," he answered. "She only seeks my opinion."

"Of course," said Mary dryly. She left the room.

William himself lately had grown uneasy. *Can it be this fashionable lady expects marriage of me?* He wrote Lady Austen two letters which affirmed his brotherly affection for her. Indignant, she destroyed them and moved to Bath in 1784.

But his correspondence with Lady Hesketh increased. He called her "Coz" (cousin) in his letters. Although domineering, she cared for him with a sister's tenderness, ensuring he had sufficient income and help in managing his affairs. William welcomed her visits to the point of obsession. She tried to calm him, yet keep his spirits up.

William and Mary also met the Throckmortons, a wealthy Catholic family who lived two miles from Olney in the village of Weston Underwood. They urged William and Mary to visit often and eventually offered them Weston Lodge, a bigger, more pleasant home near them.

Lady Hesketh helped the two relocate, managing money, furniture, and staff for William and the aging Mary. William wrote John Newton he enjoyed his new surroundings: "I am now as happy at Olney as I expect to be anywhere without the presence of God."[13]

The year 1786 proved difficult for William and Mary. William received devastating letters from John Newton regarding his and Mary's alleged sexual relationship, as rumors reached their friend's ears. William responded that some of their neighbors, ignorant and envious, twisted their actions. He also gave pained assurances of their virtue: "You may be assured, that, notwithstanding all rumors to the contrary, we are exactly what we were when you saw us last:—I, miserable on account of God's departure from me, which I believe to be final; and she seeking his return to me in the path of duty and by continual prayer."[14] Despite the temporary rift, William and Newton continued as lifelong friends.

His close relationship with Harriet Hesketh helped William fight his increasing despondency: "God grant that our friendship. . .may glow in us to our last hour, and be renewed in a better world, there to be perpetuated forever. For you must know, that I should not love you half so well, if I did not believe you would be my friend to eternity. There is not room enough for friendship to unfold itself in full bloom in such a nook of life as this."[15]

He wrote her that his own poetic abilities helped him cope: "Set me down, therefore, my dear, for an industrious rhymer, so long as I shall have the ability. For in this only way is it possible for me, so far as I can see, either to honour God, or to serve man, or even to serve myself."[16]

William Unwin died near the end of the year, deepening William's hopelessness. Despite her own grief at the loss of her son and her ill health, Mary nursed William through yet another bout of severe depression.

Although his days and nights overflowed with dark, negative

images and fear of God, William could still experience His goodness through nature as he viewed Mr. Pomfret's (his neighbor's) flower beds, "a fine bed of tulips, a sight that I never saw. Fine painting, and God the artist."[17] He considered animal sounds music created by God: "All the sounds that nature utters are delightful. . .from the gnat's fine treble to the bass of the humble bee, I admire them all. . . . Even the ears that are deaf to the Gospel are continually entertained, though without knowing it, by sounds for which they are solely indebted to its Author."[18]

Echoes of his Olney hymns lit a candle in the gray, colorless fogs that tried to conquer his days:

Sometimes a light surprises
    The Christian while he sings;
It is the Lord who rises
    With healing in his wings;
When comforts are declining,
    He grants the soul again
A season of clear shining
    To cheer it after rain.[19]

five

W hy should thousands, millions of poor Africans suffer because of the greed of my own countrymen?" demanded William, pointing to his newspaper. Mary nodded but said nothing, as his outrage (and his dyspepsia) only increased if she responded.

William had celebrated England's decree against slavery in 1772, but British slave traders still carried on their merciless, lucrative commerce abroad. The more William read of slavery, the more it revolted him. Despite his mental struggles and inactivity in politics, in 1788 William wrote "Pity for the Poor Africans" and "The Negro's Complaint" to oppose the British slave trade:

> Men from England bought and sold me,
> Paid my price in paltry gold;
> But, though slave they have enroll'd me
> Minds are never to be sold.[1]

Advocates of freedom set these verses to well-known tunes so they could be sung across Great Britain. These songs of protest helped fuel England's ultimate abolition of the slave trade in the 1830s.

Despite William's fame, he became more and more reclusive. He managed to finish a translation of poems by the Greek poet Homer, which he had begun in 1785, and published them in 1790. William then began to translate John Milton's poetry, which he never completed, as his depression made it difficult for him to concentrate.

In the midst of his stresses, his cousin Rose Bodham gave him an unexpected gift that illuminated his difficult days with loving memories.

"William, I found this in the garret this past week and thought you should have it," said Mrs. Bodham.

He stared at the picture in unbelief. His mother, long dead, smiled at him from the frame.

"You resemble her, William, although you are now almost sixty and your mother was only thirty when this was painted. I always believed you took after the Donnes," said his cousin.

Tears filled his throat so he could not answer. Mrs. Bodham patted him gently on the arm and left. William took the portrait to his bedroom and kissed it with reverence. He hung it on the wall by his bedside. *Now she will be the last thing I see before I sleep, and the first when I awake.* He took up a quill and began to write "On the Receipt of My Mother's Picture Out of Norfolk":

Faithful remembrancer of one so dear,
O welcome guest, though unexpected here:
Who bidst me honor with an artless song,
Affectionate, a mother lost so long.

Time has but half succeeded in his theft—
Thyself removed, thy power to soothe me left.[2]

The portrait of William's mother sustained him as he watched Mary's health deteriorate. She had cared for him during his most depressed periods with affection, patience, and fortitude. Now old age had begun to ravage his dear companion. Mary suffered several strokes, resulting in paralysis and severe speech impediment, as well as a personality change. When Mary demanded only William assume her care, he nursed her tenderly, night and day. William poured his agony into a poem:

> *The twentieth year is well nigh past*
> *Since first our sky was overcast;*
> *Ah! Would that this might be the last!*
>   *My Mary!*

> *Thy spirits have a fainter flow,*
> *I see thee daily weaker grow;*
> *'Twas my distress that brought thee low,*
>   *My Mary!*

> *And still to love, though press'd with ill,*
> *In wintry age to feel no chill,*
> *With me is to be lovely still,*
>   *My Mary!*[3]

His gifted, loving young cousin, John Johnson, whom William had called the "wild boy"[4] because of his joyous, uninhibited celebration of life, had written William frequently, asking his opinion about his poetry. Both enjoyed their discussions of literature. But now, William and Mary's state concerned Johnson.

William also began to cultivate the friendship of William Hayley, his biographer, who invited him and Mary to his idyllic estate in Eartham in August 1792. In the beautiful country setting, Mary recovered somewhat, and William's spirits rose enough to comfort a friend, Rev. Hurdis, in his misfortune: "The stroke [of discipline], severe as it is, is not the stroke of an enemy, but of a father. . . . Thousands have been able to say, and myself as loud as any of them, it has been good for me that I was afflicted. . . . May the Comforter of all the afflicted, who seek him, be yours. God bless you!"[5]

Although improved after his stay with Hayley, he wrote Lady Hesketh that his depression would never leave him: "It is my companion for life, and nothing will ever divorce us."[6]

As Mary worsened upon their arrival home, William's mental state deteriorated. He wrote his friends of increasing depression and horrible nightmares about thunder, lightning, graveyards, and corpses. Worst of all, he had recurring nightmares about preparations being made for his own execution by fire. His friends, including Samuel Teedon, an Olney schoolmaster who had become his spiritual counselor, pronounced such manifestations satanic. But William claimed God Himself had lodged them in his mind like a tormenting saber.

Alarmed at his letters' tone, Lady Hesketh, now widowed, arrived at Weston to care for William and Mary; she remained for months. But her own health suffered, so John Johnson, now a clergyman, decided to care for the elderly pair himself in Norfolk. Mary's health continued to deteriorate, and in December 1796, William held her hand for the last time before she died. Dr. Johnson, thinking to spare his distraught cousin, had her buried during the night without his presence. But after a brief outburst, William seemed to lose all memory of his former companion of many years. He showed no overt signs of grief for Mary and did not speak of her again. William remained mute for several weeks and ate almost nothing. In the months afterwards, he exhibited less and less emotion. He took little pleasure in his surroundings, writing Lady Hesketh that the nature he had always loved, even the ocean, had become "an universal blank to me, and though from a different cause, yet with an effect as difficult to remove, as blindness itself."[7] He wrote a farewell to John Newton, apologizing for ignoring his letters: "Adieu, dear sir, whom in those days I called dear friend, with feelings that justified the appellation."[8]

His last poem, "The Castaway," reflected his despair:

No voice divine the storm allay'd,
No light propitious shone;
When snatch'd from all effectual aid,
We perish'd each alone:

> *But I beneath rougher sea,*
> *And whelm'd in deeper gulfs than he."*[9]

William died on April 25, 1800, at sixty-nine, convinced to the end that God's Spirit had left him. Medical authorities of the latter twentieth century would diagnose him as suffering from atypical bipolar disorder because his periods of exaggerated joy were never as intense or as long as his episodes of depression. They would regard William's spontaneous remissions, his extreme feelings of guilt, suicidal tendencies, hallucinations, and emotional/social detachment near the end of his life as confirming evidence. With no effective medicines or therapies available in the 1700s, William's horrible disease seemed to conquer him, dragging him down to eternal hopelessness.

John Newton, his lifelong friend and spiritual mentor, preached his friend's funeral. He, too, spoke of William's endless struggles with mental illness. But he also spoke of his true conversion and Christian lifestyle during the many years they were neighbors: "I never in all my life saw a man walk—I want to say so honorably—but so closely with God and always set the Lord before him in all he did. . . . I don't know a person upon earth I consult upon a text of Scripture or any point of conscience so much to my satisfaction as Mr. Cowper. He could give comfort though he could not receive any himself."[10]

Newton had hoped William's deathbed experience would assure him of his salvation, but the poet had lain oblivious to his surroundings during the last hours of his life. Grieved but undismayed, John Newton anticipated his friend's unspeakable delight when he made his final escape from lifetime suffering. He wrote a few days after William's death: "Oh, with what a surprise of joy would he find himself immediately before the throne, and in the presence of his Lord! All his sorrows left below, and earth exchanged for heaven."[11]

Newton's words of hope echoed William Cowper's own when he authored "Light Shining Out of Darkness" ("God Moves in a Mysterious Way"), the last of the Olney hymns he wrote as the relentless storm of depression descended on him after the deaths of his brother John and William Unwin:

> *God moves in a mysterious way*
> *His wonders to perform;*
> *He plants His footsteps in the sea*
> *And rides upon the storm.*
>
> *You fearful saints, fresh courage take:*
> *The clouds you so much dread*
> *Are big with mercy, and shall break*
> *In blessings on your head.*
>
> *Judge not the Lord by feeble sense,*
> *But trust Him for His grace;*
> *Behind a frowning providence*
> *Faith sees a smiling face.*[12]

Despite the horrors of his earthly life, Cowper left a living legacy of hymns and poetry permeated with his faith in Jesus Christ, words that have endured well over two centuries.

The true Light penetrated the darkness of William Cowper's pain. It still shines, and the darkness has not overcome it.

NOTES

Chapter One

1. William Cowper, *The Life and Works of William Cowper*, ed. T. S. Grimshawe (Boston: Phillips, Sampson, and Company, 1856), 552.
2. William Cowper, *The Works of William Cowper, Esq.*, ed. Robert Southey, vol. 2 (London: Baldwin and Cradock, 1836), 28; letter to William Unwin, 27 May 1782.
3. Cowper, ed. Grimshawe, 620.
4. Ibid., 468.
5. Ibid., 26.
6. Ibid., 251; letter to Lady Hesketh, 17 April 1786.
7. Ibid., 469.
8. Ibid., 480.

Chapter Two

1. William Cowper, *The Poetical Works of William Cowper*, ed. John Bruce, vol. 3 (London: Bell and Daldy, 18—), 340–341.
2. Cowper, ed. Grimshawe, 474.
3. Ibid.
4. Ibid., 476.
5. Ibid., 680.
6. Ibid., 32; letter to Lady Hesketh, 4 July 1765.
7. Ibid., 31.
8. Ibid., 67; letter to William Unwin, 8 May 1780.
9. Ibid., 46; letter to Mrs. Cowper, his cousin, 14 March 1767.
10. Ibid., 45; letter to Mrs. Cowper, 3 September 1766.

Chapter Three

1. Cowper, ed. Grimshawe, 220; letter to John Newton, May 1785.
2. Ibid., 142; letter to William Unwin, 18 November 1782.
3. "The Life of William Cowper," *The Complete Poetical Works of William Cowper* in Christian Classics Ethereal Library [on-line] (Boston: Gould and Lincoln, 18—[cited 22 April 2003]); available from www.ccel.org/c/cowper/works/life.htm.
4. William Cowper, *The Works of William Cowper, Esq.*, ed. Robert Southey, vol. 5 (London: Baldwin and Cradock, 1836), 345; letter to John Newton, July 1786.
5. Cowper, ed. Grimshawe, 221.
6. Ibid., 28; letter to Lady Hesketh, 9 August 1763.
7. Ibid., 670.
8. Ibid., 676.
9. Ibid., 673.

10. "John Newton" in Christian Classics Ethereal Library [on-line] [cited 9 June 2003]; available from www.ccel.org/s/southern_ harmony/sharm/sharm/hymn/t= New+Britain.html.

11. Cowper, ed. Grimshawe, "True and False Comforts," 683.

12. Ibid., 677.

13. Ibid., 670–671.

14. Ibid., 102; letter to John Newton, 21 August 1781.

Chapter Four

1. Cowper, ed. Grimshawe, 102; letter to John Newton, 21 August 1781.

2. Ibid., 98; letter to John Newton, 12 July 1781.

3. Ibid., 102; letter to John Newton, 21 August 1781.

4. Ibid., 195–196; letter to William Unwin, 13 July 1784.

5. Ibid., 142; letter to Joseph Hill, November 1782.

6. Ibid., 153; letter to William Unwin, 8 June 1783.

7. Ibid., 270; letter to William Unwin, date unknown.

8. Ibid., 143; letter to William Unwin, 18 November 1782.

9. "The Life of William Cowper" in Christian Classics Ethereal Library [on-line].

10. Cowper, ed. Grimshawe, 564.

11. Ibid., 577.

12. Ibid., 594.

13. Ibid., 265; letter to John Newton, 5 August 1786.

14. Ibid., 272; letter to John Newton, 30 September 1786.

15. Ibid., 259.

16. Ibid., 255; letter to Lady Hesketh, 15 May 1786.

17. Ibid., 220; letter to John Newton, May 1785.

18. Ibid., 200; letter to John Newton, 18 September 1784.

19. Ibid., "Joy and Peace in Believing," 681.

Chapter Five

1. Cowper, ed. Grimshawe, "The Negro's Complaint," 618.

2. Ibid., 626.

3. Ibid., 649.

4. Ibid., 339; letter to Lady Hesketh, 22 January 1790.

5. William Hayley, *The Life and Letters of William Cowper* (London: J. Johnson and Company, 1812), 8–9; letter to Rev. Hurdis, 26 August 1792.

6. Cowper, ed. Grimshawe, 416; letter to Lady Hesketh, 26 August 1792.

7. Hayley, 164; letter to Lady Hesketh, October 1798.

8. William Cowper, *The Works of William Cowper, Esq.*, ed. Robert Southey, vol. 7 (London: Baldwin and Cradock, 1836), 253.
9. Cowper, ed. Grimshawe, 649.
10. Richard Cecil, *The Life of John Newton*, ed. Marylynn Rouse (Fearn, Ross-shire, Great Britain: Christian Focus Publications, 2000), 363–364.
11. Ibid., 283.
12. Cowper, ed. Grimshawe, 685.

Suggested Reading

"Benjamin Franklin." *Columbia Encyclopedia.* 6th ed. New York: Columbia University Press, 2002. On-line. Cited 9 June 2003. Available from www.bartleby.com/65/fr/FranklinB.htm.

Cecil, Richard, *The Life of John Newton.* Edited by Marylynn Rouse. Fearn, Ross-shire, Great Britain: Christian Focus Publications, 2000.

Cowper and Newton Museum Home Page. On-line. Cited 21 April 2003. Available from www.mkheritage.co.uk/cnm/htmlpages/cowperbiog1.html.

Cowper, William, *The Life and Works of William Cowper.* Edited by T. S. Grimshawe. Boston: Phillips, Sampson, and Company, 1856.

Cowper, William, *The Poetical Works of William Cowper.* Edited by John Bruce. Vol. 3. London: Bell and Daldy, 18—.

Cowper, William, *The Works of William Cowper, Esq.,* Edited by Robert Southey. Vols. 2, 5, 7. London: Baldwin and Cradock, 1836.

Hayley, William, *The Life and Letters of William Cowper.* London: J. Johnson and Company, 1812.

"The Inns of Court." In Online Law: Lawyers on the Web. On-line. Cited 26 June 2003. Available at www.online-law.co.uk/bar/inns_of_court.html.

"The Life of William Cowper." *The Complete Poetical Works of William Cowper.* Boston: Gould and Lincoln, 18—. In Christian Classics Ethereal Library. On-line. Cited 22 April 2003. Available from www.ccel.org/c/cowper/works/life.htm.

Meyer, Joachim-Ernst and Ruth Meyer, "Self-Portrayal by a Depressed Poet: A Contribution to the Clinical Biography of William Cowper." *American Journal of Psychiatry* 144:2 (February 1987): 127–32.

Newton, John, "Amazing Grace." In Christian Classics Ethereal Library. On-line. Cited 9 June 2003. Available from www.ccel.org/s/southern_harmony/sharm/sharm/hymn/t=New+Britain.html.

Ryskamp, Charles, *William Cowper of the Inner Temple, Esq.* Great Britain: Cambridge University Press, 1959.

Van Doren, Mark, *The Selected Letters of William Cowper.* New York: Farrar, Straus, and Young, Inc., 1951.

FRANCES
HAVERGAL

one

F anny, where are you?"

The mother scanned the gardens that sprawled beyond the window. Her youngest daughter loved to climb trees and play in the rose garden near the Anglican parsonage in Astley, England, where they lived. But on this June morning in 1844, she saw no sign of the blond, fairylike child.

"Fanny, dear, you must show yourself!"

Mrs. Havergal heard a slight noise behind her and peered under her parlor table. Mischievous blue eyes met her gaze.

"There you are! Come, Frances."

The child scrambled from her hiding place, hauling her heavy books with her. When her mother called her by her full name, instant obedience was in order. Her favorite playmate, a spotted tan-and-white spaniel named Flora, also rose with a bark.

Jane Havergal tried not to smile. "Little Quicksilver," as Fanny's minister father called her, could charm her way out of difficulties with one winsome grin. "The German master will soon arrive to tutor the other children. You must play outdoors."

"Oh, but may I not stay in the library and listen, Mama?"

Mrs. Havergal's eyebrows went up. Usually her active daughter welcomed every opportunity to spend time in the garden.

"I will read these books while he teaches them. I will pet

Flo; we will be oh, so quiet! Please?"

Most seven year olds could not remain still during lessons, Mrs. Havergal knew. But Fanny had begun reading simple books at age three; at four she could read the Bible and print. Despite her liveliness, she possessed a rare ability to concentrate that exceeded that of her older siblings—that is, when she wanted to!

"Flo," said her mother with a decided gesture, "must go outside—"

"Oh, but Flo wants to learn German! I've already taught her 'Come!' and 'Lie down!' in French."

"Then she may learn German the same way—from you, privately!" Jane clasped the wriggling animal's collar and called for the scullery boy to escort her out the back door of the parsonage.

Fanny sighed but darted into the library before her mother could change her mind. Her teenaged sister, also named Jane, smiled as Fanny took her place on a little stool near the fireplace. "So you are joining us today, Fanny."

Jane had begun giving her music lessons. "Have you practiced your piano lesson?"

"All three songs," said Fanny. "I love the sonatina!"

"But you haven't finished your writing exercises!" said Henry.

Fanny did not enjoy her older brother's rigorous instruction. "I finished them after breakfast," she retorted.

"You're just afraid she'll learn more German than you," said Frank to his brother with a wicked smile. The youngest of her siblings, Frank, sometimes teamed with Fanny to annoy Henry.

"*Guten Tag*," said Herr Josef, their instructor, interrupting the budding argument. "Today we will study the nouns."

The children opened their books, and for an hour Fanny sat entranced. She took care, however, to fix her eyes on her storybook and turn pages occasionally. *If Henry knows I'm learning German faster than he is, he might ask Mama to make me stay outside.*

A few days later, Fanny called Flo in a loud whisper: "*Gekommen.*" The spaniel bounded to her small mistress with a joyous bark. "Good dog! You are learning German, too," said Fanny, "but we shan't let Henry know, shall we?" She patted the animal, who stared at her with adoring eyes.

Fanny's growing knowledge did not remain a secret long. A few months later, the German master heard the child singing a German song in her sweet, clear soprano as she played in the garden.

"Can it be? She has learned the song, beginning to finish, as well as the others!" marveled Herr Josef. He considered himself fortunate in teaching the Havergal children; gifted and eager, they were delightful pupils. "But the little one, she sings German as if it were her native language! And such a lovely voice!" On impulse, he called over the fence, "*Gekommenes, kleines Mädchen. Wir müssen heute studieren* [Come, little girl. We must study today]."

Her little face beamed with joy. "*Wunderbar! Lassen Sie uns gehen, Herr Josef!* [Wonderful! Let us go, Herr Josef]," she answered.

His eyes widened as they conversed in German all the way to the door. When they encountered Henry in the hallway, Fanny suddenly fell silent. But her brother, shaking his head, grinned and scooped her up in his arms.

"So—you will surpass me in German," Henry admitted. "But your penmanship still needs a great deal of practice!"

Fanny spent a happy early childhood at the various parishes where her father, Rev. William Henry Havergal, served. Born Frances Ridley Havergal on December 14, 1836, in Astley, Worcestershire, she and her five siblings gained a love of music, poetry, and other intellectual pursuits from their father. Rev. Havergal was an accomplished musician and composer who donated earnings from his published works to missionary causes and church repairs within his denomination. Fanny loved to sit on her father's lap during family worship and listen to his strong voice as he sang the great hymns of the church. When he read daily Scriptures to his family, she tried to follow the words with her finger. Later, her sister Maria noted, "It is likely that she learned to read as a mere pastime."[1]

Fanny and her brothers and sisters also flourished in the

spiritual climate their parents created. Both Rev. Havergal and his wife loved and served Jesus Christ with their quiet, precise lifestyle. They enjoyed Bible studies and prayer meetings. Even when Fanny was quite small, her mother expressed fervent hope her little daughter would become a Christian.

In this positive atmosphere, seven-year-old Fanny wrote her first poem:

> Sunday is a pleasant day,
>   When we to church do go;
> For there we sing and read and pray,
>   And hear the sermon too.
>
> On Sunday hear the village bells;
>   It seems as if they said,
> Go to the church where the pastor tells
>   How Christ for man has bled.
>
> And if we love to pray and read
>   While we are in our youth,
> The Lord will help us in our need
>   And keep us in His truth.[2]

When her older siblings left home for boarding school and marriage, Fanny wrote them often. She even sent letters to Frank and to her friends composed entirely of lines that rhymed!

Active, joyous, and charming, the little girl appeared to live a carefree life. But one Sunday morning, she heard a visiting minister's sermon that shook her to the depths of her young soul.

"Revelation 14:10 tells us, 'The same shall drink of the wine of the wrath of God, which is poured out without mixture into the cup of his indignation; and he shall be tormented with fire and brimstone in the presence of the holy angels, and in the presence of the Lamb'!" roared the clergyman.

Fanny shrank into the corner of the pew. Her father had never preached this way. The minister's black eyes, glittering with rage, pierced her trembling heart. Almost any moment, she felt certain God's fire would erupt from his mouth like the pictures of the dragon in a storybook she read at home. Fanny could feel the searing heat of God's rage, smell the brimstone that would surely explode in the sanctuary, destroying sinners like her—sinners who stole sweet biscuits from her mother's pantry.

When she survived the service, Fanny breathed a sigh of relief. Her fledgling faith hardened into meticulous legalism. She made sure every Sunday afternoon she read a chapter of the Bible and prayed. If she were faithful in her spiritual exercises, would God forgive her if she took only the *littlest* biscuit? Her careful religious activities bored her beyond measure, as did her parents' attempts to instruct her in the Christian faith. But Fanny persisted in her rituals, although she feared even her most intense sacrifices would not dispel God's wrath. She secretly decided to enjoy her sinful moments while she could.

But her parents' fragrant rose garden, the trees' green, inviting arms, the china blue sky, and truant clouds all spoke to her of her Maker's goodness. All her life Fanny cherished the outdoors. As a child she read William Cowper's nature poetry and longed to become a Christian: "Oh if God would but make me a Christian before the summer comes!"[3] But she felt unworthy of God's attention. At the St. Nicholas parsonage, she often retreated to her room, pondering her desire for God yet her inability to obey Him.

I must pray very hard so God will change me, Fanny decided. But no real sense of faith assured her God would respond to her prayers. Later Fanny wrote, "As for *trying* to be good, that seemed of next to no use; it was like struggling in a quicksand, the more you struggle, the deeper you sink."[4]

Once, the child decided to share her inner turmoil with a kindly, neighboring pastor. He answered her with ill-concealed amusement: "Fanny, child, you are upset because of your removal from a dear, familiar home in the country to a new town. One always misses one's former playmates. Within a month or two, you will make new friends and feel at home here." He patted her on the head, which Fanny hated.

Such a simplistic view of her feelings angered Fanny. She resolved never to share her uncertainties with anyone again.

But she took more interest in the church liturgy than ever before. The idea of Communion, in particular, fascinated Fanny. Not allowed to attend, she hid in the church vestry and listened to the service, tears running down her face. *Do I dare believe some day I will become a Christian?*

When Fanny turned eleven, she finally gained the opportunity to observe Communion when her mother became ill and was served the sacrament at home.

Mama does not appear any better after taking Communion, thought Fanny. Her mother had been ill for months. Fanny had hoped the holy ritual would put color in Mrs. Havergal's faded cheeks and ease the lines of pain and exhaustion that creased her face more each day. *But she does seem happier afterwards.*

"Fanny! Mother wishes to speak with you," said Jane, finding her little sister in her room pondering the clouds and writing.

Fanny raced to the forbidden sickroom, hungry for her mother's touch.

Jane caught her before she scampered through the door. "Fanny!" she said sharply. "Mother is—is—" Jane's voice failed her, and her large eyes filled with tears. Fanny stopped short, puzzled.

"You must be very, very quiet, dear," said Jane, hugging her. "Mother cannot bear too much. . . ."

Fanny crept into her mother's room, her face filled with alarm. Despite her pain, the sick woman smiled at the sight of the child.

"Fanny, you need not tiptoe," she said, raising emaciated arms. Fanny ran to her bedside, where her mother held her as if she would never let go.

Fanny prattled of favorite stories. She read poems to her mother that she had written in her little journal. Mrs. Havergal savored every word, her thin face glowing as it did after taking Communion. But her eye held a resigned look Fanny could not endure. She chattered faster and louder until her mother raised a wasted hand and laid it on her head.

"Fanny, dear, I must tell you something important," she said when Fanny paused for breath. The young girl backed away. "And you shall listen," said her mother in a resolute tone. Fanny sat down on a stool beside the bed.

"I shall not recover while on this earth," said Mrs. Havergal. "Before many days I shall meet my Savior and go to live in heaven with Him."

Fanny stared at her mother, blank, unhearing.

The exhausted woman fell back on her pillows, her strength ebbing as she struggled to speak. "Fanny, dear, pray to God to prepare you for all that He is preparing for you.[5] I do pray for the Holy Spirit to lead you and guide you. And remember, nothing but the precious blood of Christ can make you clean and lovely in God's sight."[6]

Fanny buried her head in her mother's chest and lay motionless. Mrs. Havergal stroked her head with trembling hands until Jane entered and took her from the sickroom.

Her sister Maria, weeping, tried to comfort Fanny, but the young girl pulled away.

"Sick people always get better in the beautiful summer," said Fanny, her eyes dry, her face defiant.

"They often do," said Maria, "but—"

Fanny ran outside and climbed a tree in their tiny garden, remaining among its comforting branches until tea.

No matter how her sisters tried to reason with Fanny, she ignored their attempts to prepare her for Mrs. Havergal's death. Even as her mother weakened, then grew comatose, Fanny refused to accept her demise. When the suffering woman died on July 5, 1848, Fanny, who had heard of resuscitations after apparent deaths, expected her mother to rise from her coffin in the parlor. When she did not, the young girl ran to her room and wept for hours, spilling hundreds of tears into the pillow her mother had embroidered during happier days. Then, resolved to carry on Mrs. Havergal's faith, Fanny dipped her quill into the inkwell and wrote:

Eye hath not seen, nor ear hath heard,
Neither can man's heart conceive,
The blessed things God hath prepared
For those who love Him and believe.[7]

Her family was relieved to see her acknowledge her mother's death. Fanny made a gradual return to the life she had always known: voracious hours of reading and writing, walks in the crisp autumn air, services in her father's church. But dark grief often found her at night. And although God's generosity in sending His Son for her sins became a reality to her, Fanny despaired of her imperfections. "I couldn't expect a happier lot than I had, and yet all I had was unsatisfactory; and I should always be *myself* too, and I hated my*self*, so what was to be done?"[8]

On January 1, 1850, when village bells rang in the New Year and a new decade, thirteen-year-old Fanny lay awake, thinking. *When 1860 arrives, I shall be an adult, if I live. Will I be a Christian? If I die, where will I be?*

"Your hat is tilted sideways," said Maria to Fanny.

"Oh, fix it, do!" answered Fanny. She was too excited at the prospect of going to Mrs. Teed's boarding school at Belmont to adjust her bonnet. She had studied extensively at home but knew few girls her own age. Some children dreaded boarding school, but Fanny could hardly wait for the adventure to begin!

She missed her family and her quiet room at home, but she enjoyed the challenging classes. The school required the girls to speak French at all times, and Fanny, who loved studying languages, was in her element. The caring teachers, the luxury of new friends, and the hustle and bustle of well-organized dormitory life opened a new world for the wide-eyed young girl. Mrs. Teed, a kind and fervent Christian, made no secret of her goal for her students: by Christmas, she hoped each would profess faith in Christ. She encouraged teachers to hold prayer meetings. Conversions became an everyday occurrence.

Fanny savored the electric atmosphere, longing to connect

with the faith that charged everyone but herself. Her best friend, Diana, testified of her new life in Christ. When Fanny confided her doubts to her friend Mary, she pleaded with Fanny to be honest with God. "Tell Him you find it impossible to love Him, and He will help you learn," she assured Fanny, whose longing for God only intensified. She read Psalm 42:1–2, "As the hart panteth after the water brooks, so panteth my soul after thee, O God. My soul thirsteth for God, for the living God: when shall I come and appear before God?"

Did King David feel as distant from You as I? wondered Fanny.

During winter recess, one of her favorite teachers, Miss Caroline Ann Cooke, visited her at Jane's Oakhampton home. One snowy Sunday evening, Fanny confessed her doubts as they sat by the crackling fire.

"I want assurance of forgiveness of my sins above everything," said Fanny, with tears in her eyes. "Above *everything*— even the love of my father and my brothers and sisters!"

Miss Cooke held her close. "Then, Fanny, I think, *I am sure*, it will not be very long before your desire is granted, your hope fulfilled. Why cannot you trust yourself to your Saviour at once? Supposing that now, at this moment, Christ were to come in the clouds of heaven, and take up His redeemed, could you not trust Him? Would not His call, His promise, be enough for you? Could you not commit your soul to Him, to your Saviour Jesus?"[9]

The young girl ran to her room, her heart pounding, her mind alive with hope. "I was very happy at last," she wrote later. "I could commit my soul to Jesus. I did not, and need not, fear His coming. I could trust Him with my all for eternity. It was so utterly new to have any bright thoughts about religion that I could hardly believe it could be so, that I had really gained such a step. Then and there, I committed my soul to the Saviour, I do not mean to say without *any* trembling or fear, but I did—and earth and heaven seemed bright from that moment—*I did trust the Lord Jesus.*"[10]

For the first time, Fanny's Sunday Scripture reading came

alive. Incomprehensible church services made sense. The dark wintry days shone bright as summer for fourteen-year-old Fanny as she celebrated the ecstasy of a clean conscience and her new intense bond with Jesus Christ.

She and Miss Cooke also grew close. As their relationship blossomed, so did Miss Cooke's new friendship with Fanny's father. The young girl's lonely heart sang for joy when Miss Caroline Cooke married Rev. Havergal in July 1851, and became her beloved stepmother.

two

I am *so* delighted to come to school!" said Fanny the following fall.[1] She hugged Miss Haynes and nearly upset her teacup. The dignified headmistress of Powick Court reacted as if a firecracker had exploded under her nose, but Fanny's ear-to-ear smile quelled her indignation at the exuberant greeting. In the following weeks, Miss Haynes would celebrate Fanny's presence with equal delight; her new student's brilliant achievements excited her teachers. No other pupil sought challenges the way Fanny Havergal did!

But a few weeks before Christmas, illness struck, and Fanny had to go home. Her high fever persisted, while problems with her eyesight forced her to avoid reading. A seeping, painful skin infection accompanied her other symptoms. Fanny, who hated inactivity, had to rest for days on end.

Her father also became ill. He and Fanny went to Colwyn, North Wales, to recover. Although Fanny could not go to school, she managed to learn Welsh as she conversed with a young servant who cared for donkeys.

"Look, Father!" she said. "I found a Welsh New Testament at the booksellers! And a prayer book!"

Her father shook his head. "Frances, dear, you are to *rest*. Not study!"

Rev. Havergal had never liked "Fanny" as a nickname. As Fanny grew older, she preferred her full name as well.

"I know, Father," she answered. "But I must read the Scriptures every day! Why not in Welsh?"

Rev. Havergal could not discourage that!

Frances's eyesight and her overall health improved in Wales, but she still suffered extended periods of severe weakness.

"The doctor says you may not return to school before next year," Rev. Havergal told her, lowering his eyes. He knew he had just dashed his daughter's hopes.

"I know you wish to take good care of me," said Frances through her tears.

"If you continue to recover, you may accompany Caroline and me to Germany this fall," said Rev. Havergal. "Dr. De Leuw, a famous oculist, may be able to improve my eyesight—perhaps yours as well—and he charges those with little money small fees for his expertise."

In November 1852, Frances traveled with her father and stepmother to Grafrath, Germany, where the prominent doctor practiced. Despite the chilly weather, she enjoyed long walks in the countryside and wrote relatives about their friendly innkeeper, who kept thirteen dogs and cats: "They follow him up to bed every night; the gentle patter of fifty-two feet is extremely amusing."[2]

Frances persuaded her parents to allow her to attend school, called the Louisenschule, that winter. She soon realized the German school differed from English ones she had attended. None of the 110 students concerned themselves with religion; when Frances lived her faith in her usual forthright way, they regarded her with disdain. Some hid her schoolbooks or pens. One girl mocked Frances's fervent prayer before she ate. Most simply snubbed her, leaving Frances alone at meals and other social times.

But Frances decided such treatment presented opportunity to model Christ: "I felt I must try to walk worthy of my calling, for Christ's sake; and it brought a new and very strong desire to bear witness for my Master, to adorn His doctrine, and to win

others for Him. It made me more watchful and earnest than perhaps ever before, for I knew that any slip, in word or deed, would
bring discredit on my profession [of faith in Christ]."[3]

By the school year's end, Frances's patient endurance and
friendly smile won most of her persecutors. Her teachers, astonished at their English pupil's excellent progress, voted her *Numero
Eins*, or "Number One," an honor they had given to no foreigner
before.

Frances sometimes struggled with her deep love of learning:
"Day after day I grew more eager for my lessons, and less earnest
in seeking Jesus."[4]

When school ended, Frances went to live and study with
Pastor Schulze-Bergen and his wife in Oberkassal, a picturesque
village on the Rhine River, while her parents traveled. The pastor was a learned man who loved discussing Goethe, as well as
other German literature, composition, and history with Frances.
She often went boating on the Rhine, rowing with all her might
as castles, medieval-looking villages, and rich farmlands drifted
past. Frances met a nearby Christian nobleman, Count von
Lippe, and his family, who led a plain lifestyle because they gave
away half their income. They invited her to discuss German
writers and drink tea with them. Frances met their many aristocratic friends and relatives, and she wrote a schoolmate that one
of the countess's daughters was a princess: "I should like her to
come while I am here, as I have never spoken to a princess in my
life!"[5] After a year of living and traveling in Germany, Frances
found she could hardly think in English! She returned to
England in December 1853 to prepare for her confirmation in
the Anglican Church at age seventeen.

"My God, oh, my *own* Father, Thou blessed Jesus my *own*
Saviour, Thou Holy Spirit my *own* Comforter,"[6] prayed Frances
as she awaited the ritual of confirmation. She drew in a sharp
breath and glanced at Ellen Wakeman, who had walked with her
in the procession to the church. Had Ellen heard her bold pre-
sumption? But Ellen remained silent, her eyes closed.

Why do I concern myself with Ellen's response? Should I not fear

God, who knows the weakness of my Christian life? Frances's heart hammered, yet she could not recant her passionate prayer.

Dr. Henry Pepys, Bishop of Worcester, asked the candidates to affirm their faith and obedience to Christ.

The Lord is your strength. The Lord is your strength. The words stroked Frances's tense mind, eased her taut, anxious heart. She answered the clergyman in a low whisper: "Lord, I cannot without Thee, but oh, with Thy almighty help—I DO."[7]

She knelt before the bishop. His strong, gentle hands rested on her head: "Defend, O Lord, this Thy child with Thy heavenly grace, that she may continue Thine for ever, and daily increase in Thy Holy Spirit more and more, until she come into Thy everlasting kingdom."[8]

Thine—forever, Lord? A tiny fountain of joy erupted deep inside Frances. "But I still rather sadly wished that I could *feel* more," she wrote later.[9]

The bishop's final benediction calmed Frances's uncertainties. "Why should I doubt that my soul will indeed receive the blessing which God's minister is thus giving? Why did God appoint him thus to bless if it were to be a mere idle form?"[10] Later that day, July 17, 1854, she wrote a short poem containing the bishop's words that had reverberated throughout her soul:

> Oh, "Thine for ever," what a blessed thing
> To be for ever His who died for me!
> My Saviour, all my life Thy praise I'll sing,
> Nor cease my song throughout eternity.[11]

"How wonderful to be at home again!" said Frances. She had moved to a larger bedroom in the St. Nicholas parsonage, but she often studied in her former room, watching feathery gray clouds pass her window as she pondered the Greek vocabulary her father had begun teaching her. Frances pored over her Greek New Testament, exploring new scriptural insights and making detailed notes.

She also wrote poems in German and English, including

playful charades and enigmas. Both literary forms were complex riddles in rhyme, and Frances enjoyed confounding her relatives and friends with them.

"Your sister has written a new enigma for Maria's birthday!" said Rev. Havergal as the family finished their plum cake. "Can we solve the riddle before we retire?"

"The last one took two days!" said Frank. "Perhaps Frances should publish them so she can keep the English populace occupied with her riddles and therefore not employed in mischief!"

Frances's blue eyes twinkled wickedly, but she stood and read her latest creation as her family pondered and grimaced:

> *I am the child of the brightest thing*
> *   Which may gladden mortal eyes,*
> *Yet the silent sweep of my dusty wing*
> *Over my mother may dimness fling,*
> *   And smiling she faints and dies.*
>
> *I move, I dance, I fall, I fly,*
> *   Yet anon I may calmly sleep;*
> *I mark the bright-winged hours flit by,*
> *Your ingenuity perhaps I try;*
> *   I am long, or short, or deep.*
>
> *All the day through I follow you*
> *   Yet beware how you follow me;*
> *For each child of man I may oft beguile,*
> *And cloud the light of his sunniest smile,*
> *   Till for ever away I flee.*[12]

"What on earth can it be?" muttered Jane. She was expecting her second child and sometimes grew a little cross at night.

Maria patted her shoulder. "We shall solve this one in a more timely manner." She mused, "Hmm. . .'the silent sweep of my dusty wing'—and the mother dies. Could it be the shadow of death?"

"I believe," said Henry before Frances could answer, "that she is speaking of shadows in general. Am I right, Frances?"

"Correct! You are all far too intelligent," said Frances, "and I am far too merciful! When you complained about my last enigma, I designed this easy one! You shall regret your quick answer!"

The family laughed and teased her, but Frank said, "Fanny, any publisher would welcome your poetry. It is truly excellent."

Frances blushed. "I hesitate to spend my energies on such light verse, Frank, and I question whether I should provide others with opportunity to waste theirs!"

"Surely our good times are not a waste, Fanny," said Frank. "Other families as well would benefit from your poems!"

Frances respected her brother's opinion, especially as he was now himself a pastor. She sent several enigmas and charades to a publisher, requesting, should he use her works, that he publish them under pseudonyms: "Sabrina" and "Zoide." He complied, selling her poems in small booklets called "pocket books," the forerunners of paperbacks.

When Frances showed Frank published copies of her poems and the company's check, Frank threw his hat into the air and cheered. "I knew you could do it, Fanny!"

Frances handed him the money. "You inspired me; therefore, my first check will go to your church missionary society. I have no pressing needs, and God's missionaries do."

three

I have the same sins and temptations as before, and I do not strive against them more than before, and it is often just as hard work. But, whereas I could not see why I *should* be saved, I now cannot see why I should not be saved if Christ died for all. On that word I take my stand and *rest there*."[1]

After her confirmation, Frances enjoyed more security in her relationship with Christ and kept busy as ever.

Frances continued to cherish her family. She made her home with her father and stepmother but often visited her siblings, especially Jane and her husband, Henry Crane. For some years she taught her small nieces, Evelyn and Constance, until they departed for boarding school. She loved her siblings' children, teaching them lessons and riding horses, swimming, skating, and playing croquet and chess with them.

Several Christian men attempted to court Frances, but her devotion remained with her extended family and her studies and ministry.

Frances delved into languages. She learned Hebrew, Latin, and sign language for the deaf and advanced her knowledge of Greek, French, and German. She studied Italian, utilizing stray moments as she schooled her nieces. Frances wrote later: "I know, by my own teaching days, how very much might be learnt in all the odds and ends of time, how *(e.g.)* I learnt all the Italian verbs while my nieces were washing their hands for dinner after our walk, because I could be ready in five minutes less time than they could."[2]

She did not neglect her spiritual life, praying four times a day and keeping copious notes of Bible studies. During her lifetime Frances memorized all the Gospels, the Epistles, Revelation, Psalms, the Minor Prophets, and the book of Isaiah, one of her favorites.

Frances also used her time to minister to others. She loved teaching children in Sunday school, despite several challenging classes. Frances kept a detailed prayer journal of her pupils' backgrounds, needs, and progress for fourteen years. When she stopped teaching Sunday school, several children pleaded with her to meet them on an individual basis, as they could not imagine continuing without her friendship and spiritual care.

She visited the poor, cheering and comforting them. One lonely invalid treasured her kindness: "It was Miss Frances who first taught me Greek, which was *such* an interest and help to me, and afterwards she gave me Hebrew lessons too. Truly can I say, 'I thank my God on every remembrance of thee!' "[3]

Frances was an excellent overall musician, memorizing many piano works by Handel, Beethoven, and Mendelssohn during her lifetime. One of Beethoven's own pupils would consider her rendition of the "Moonlight Sonata" excellent. Ferdinand Hiller, the premier German composer of the time, would praise her harmonies, amazed that she had studied composition with no one other than her father. An accomplished singer, Frances also directed choirs. She not only performed solos in concert halls and churches, but also ran singing sessions in schools, often harvesting opportunities to speak to children about Jesus Christ. When Frances visited several schools on a family trip to Ireland, one young girl wrote of Frances's concert at her school: "Miss Frances, caroling like a bird, flashed into the room! Flashed! Yes, I say the word advisedly, flashed in like a burst of sunshine, like a hillside breeze, and stood before us, her fair sunny curls falling round her shoulders, her bright eyes dancing, and her fresh sweet voice ringing through the room. I shall never forget the afternoon, never! I sat perfectly spellbound as she sang chant and hymn with marvelous sweetness, and then played two or three pieces of Handel, which thrilled me through and through."[4]

One of the other schoolgirls, moved by Frances's exuberance, responded, "Lord, teach me, even me, to know and love Thee too."[5]

Since her earlier struggles with ill health at school, Frances remained vulnerable to illness. Her family tried to protect her from workaholic tendencies but sometimes threw their hands up in despair when she kept busy (as she did on the Irish journey), even when they designed trips for her rest.

On a second venture to Germany not long before her twentieth birthday, Frances visited a pastor friend in Düsseldorf. In his study she viewed a painting of Christ crowned with thorns, standing before Pilate and a howling mob. An inscription read, "This have I done for thee; what hast thou done for Me?" Frances could hardly take her eyes off the painting by Sternberg. She began to write:

I gave My life for thee,
*   My precious blood I shed*
That thou might'st ransomed be,
*   And quickened from the dead.*
I gave My life for thee;
What hast thou given for Me?

I suffered much for thee,
*   More than thy tongue may tell,*
Of bitterest agony,
*   To rescue thee from hell.*
I suffered much for thee;
What canst thou bear for Me?

Oh, let thy life be given,
*   Thy years for Him be spent,*
World-fetters all be riven,
*   And joy with suffering blent;*

183

> *I gave Myself for thee:*
> *Give thou thyself to Me!*[6]

When Frances traveled home to England, she found the poem in her handbag. She said in disgust, "Such terrible writing!" and tossed it into the fireplace.

Rev. Havergal found the scorched scrap, which had somehow floated from the flames, and read it. "Frances, have you written another version of this poem, that you should discard it?"

Frances blushed and said, "Papa, I did not bother!"

"Why not?" asked her father.

"I thought it poor and not worthy of God's notice," answered Frances.

"All our works are poor and not worthy of God's notice," said Rev. Havergal, "but despite that, we give them to Him to use as He sees fit. May I set your poem to music?"

"Certainly, Papa, if you believe it can be of some value to Him."

Rev. Havergal composed music for her lines, and the poem Frances rejected became a popular hymn. Years later, Philip Bliss would write the modern tune for "I Gave My Life for Thee."

When Rev. Havergal's health deteriorated again, he left St. Nicholas to shepherd a smaller, rural congregation at Shareshill. Although Frances had rebelled at moving to St. Nicholas, she now hated leaving the kind parishioners who had become family to her. But the Shareshill congregation made the Havergals feel at home. Frances also welcomed living in the country once more. "Perhaps we can keep a spaniel like Flo, with whom to share a good run each day!"

Despite her devotion to Christ, Frances battled feelings of spiritual insecurity: "I had hoped that a kind of table-land had been reached in my journey, where I might walk awhile in the light, without the weary succession of rock and hollow, crag and morass, stumbling and striving."[7] Her exultation in her many accomplishments troubled her: "A power utterly new and unexpected was given me [singing and composition of music]. . .and rejoicing in this I forgot the Giver and found such delight in this that other things paled before it."[8] She was relieved when ill health and limited energy prevented her from singing in public with orchestras in halls and opera houses: "The pleasure of public applause when singing in the Philharmonic concerts is not again to exercise its delicious delusion, I do thank Him who heard my prayer. But I often pray in the dark, as it were, and feel no response from above. Is this to test me?"[9]

Another serious illness at age twenty-seven forced Frances to abandon all her ministry activities for months: "I do not think I would have chosen otherwise than as He ordered it for me; but it seems as if my spiritual life would never go without weights, and I dread needing more discipline."[10] When she grew too ill to write the poetry she loved, Frances reasoned that God was testing her, preparing her to sympathize with others who struggled. But she did not find such training easy to accept: "I suppose that God's crosses are often made of most unexpected and strange material."[11] Sometimes she even despaired of her relationship with Christ: "Oh, if He would only show me 'wherefore He contendeth with me.' It has brought me to the terrible old feeling, 'how can I be one of His sheep if I never hear the Shepherd's voice?' "[12]

When Frances finally recovered and resumed her activities, her doubts lessened. "It seems as if the Lord had led me into a calmer and more equable frame of mind; not joy, but peace."[13]

Frances joined the Young Women's Christian Association in 1867, committing herself to its mission for the rest of her life. She also nurtured links with the Anglican Church missionary society, its pastoral aid society, an organization to evangelize Jews, and the Bible Society, often supporting them with her royalties.

She began writing again. Most of her poetry came to her as complete works: "All my best have come. . .full grown. It is so curious, one minute I have not an idea of writing anything, the next I *have* a poem; it is *mine,* I see it all, except laying out rhymes and metre, which is then easy work! I rarely write anything which has not come thus."[14]

At times her moralizing poems reflected her own frustrations:

> *People do not understand me,*
> *   Their ideas are not like mine.*
> *All advances seem to land me*
> *   Still outside their guarded shrine.*
>
> *'Twill not be a fruitless labor,*
> *   Overcome this ill with good;*
> *Try to understand your neighbor,*
> *   And you will be understood.*[15]

She resumed singing lessons with a Signor Randegger, who asked Frances to write an essay on the voice's anatomy and production. Sick with a small relapse, Frances amused herself by writing the assignment in rhyme:

> *Alas for the player, the pipes, and the keys,*
> *If the bellows give out an inadequate breeze!*
> *So this is the method of getting up steam,*
> *The one motive power for song or for scream.*
> *Slowly and deeply, and just like a sigh,*
> *Fill the whole chest with a mighty supply;*
> *Through the mouth only, and not through the nose;*
> *And the lungs must condense it ere farther it goes.*
> *(How to condense it I really don't know,*
> *And very much hope the next lesson will show.)*[16]

Tragedy struck Frances's family in 1868, when her sister Jane's daughter, Evelyn Crane, died of an illness. Overcome with grief, Frances wrote:

> *Dying? Evelyn, darling!*
> *Dying? Can it be?*
> *Spring so joyous all around,*
> *Such a spring, so early crowned,*
> *Heralding all summer glee,*
> *Life for everything but thee.*

Father, where the shadows fall
Deeper yet, deepest of all,
Send Thy peace, and show Thy power
In affliction's direst hour.[17]

Frances accompanied the Cranes on a trip to Switzerland soon afterward and quickly became addicted to the magnificent Alps. Early one morning she and Miriam, Evelyn's older sister, ascended to the roof of their hotel to see the first gleams of sunlight on the snowy mountains, a sight she had longed for all her life. "I am not disappointed," she wrote in her journal. "They are just as pure and bright and peace-suggestive as ever I dreamt them. It may be rather in the style of the old women who invariably say, 'It's just like heaven,' when they get a tolerably comfortable tea-meeting; but really I never saw anything material and earthly which so suggested the ethereal and heavenly, which so seemed to lead up to the unseen, to be the very steps of the Throne. . . ."[18]

She would take several trips to Switzerland. On one of these, Frances and her friend Elizabeth Clay left their hotel at 4:00 A.M. to scale Mt. Sparrenhorn, a ten-thousand-foot mountain. "In the south west the grand mountains stood, white and perfectly clear, as if they might be waiting for the resurrection, with the moon shining pale and radiant over them, the deep Rhone valley dark and grave-like in contrast below. As we got higher, the first rose flush struck the Mischabel and Weisshorn, and Monteleone came to life too; it was *real* rose-fire, delicate yet intense. . . . When the tip of the Matterhorn caught the red light on its evil-looking rocky peak, it was just like a volcano and looked rather awful than lovely, giving one the idea of an evil angel. . . . The eastern ridges were almost jet, in front of the great golden glow into which the daffodil sky heightened. By 4:30 A.M. it was all over."[19]

Frances loved to slide down the mountains in a standing or squatting position without skis, called "glissading." Small groups of tourists, roped together, often traveled down mountainsides in this manner.

On one such outing, Frances craved a more adventurous sliding path than the one the guide indicated. "This is easier than the last slope," said Frances impatiently, "and no challenge. Is there no more exciting route for us to follow, Payot?" she asked him with a disarming smile.

"Mademoiselle, the afternoon wanes; perhaps a rest is in order," said Payot.

Frances's friends, the Sneps, who were roped to Frances and Payot, had earlier advised the guide that the lively English lady sometimes forgot her delicate health and needed a little restraining.

Frances sighed but poised herself for another slide. "Come, Payot, we will lead the way!" she called and plunged down the mountain, pulling the guide after her. Snep and his wife readied themselves for the glissade, then realized in horror that Frances and the guide were sliding off course onto a steep incline. It ended in a cliff's edge!

Jesus! Jesus! Frances's legs and arms flailed helplessly as she tumbled over icy rocks. The measureless dark valley below pulled her closer, closer towards its evil maw. *Will I meet You today in the abyss?*

"Drop down!" shouted Snep. He and his wife instantly flattened themselves on their backs, digging their heels and fingers into the snow's crust.

Frances felt the rope's sharp jerk on her waist; for a moment she could not breathe. She clawed at the snow and felt herself finally stop. Frances lay prone, too bruised and exhausted to move.

"Mademoiselle Havergal! Beware!" Payot somehow scrambled to her side. "We are very close to the edge! Only the good God and Monseiur Snep saved us today!" He helped her sit up, then stand. Frances stared through the gray mists at the tiny trees and houses far below. She gave a shaky laugh. "Well, Payot, God has decreed we linger on this earth!"

"So it seems, mademoiselle." The man lowered his eyes. "I am sorry; I, too, underestimated the route."

"Nonsense, Payot. We should not have endangered ourselves if I had not been so careless! Pulling you all toward this precipice!" Frances shook her head.

"We are safe. Let us go thank Monsieur Snep for his assistance!" The wiry little man took Frances's arm.

"Thanks be to God," said Snep.

"Amen!" said his wife, and she hugged Frances. No one said anything more. Payot led them to a sheltered spot behind large boulders, and the party rested.

"We return to Chamonix now," said Payot.

Frances protested. "But according to regulations, we may slide for four more hours!"

"But, mademoiselle—" the guide stared at her, chagrined.

"I told you!" said Snep. "Frances is not easily swayed from her purposes!"

"May we slide for only one more hour? Perhaps two? I shall really take care this time," said Frances. "But we soon will leave Switzerland, and I *must* enjoy my glissades while I may!"

So Frances and the Sneps, undeterred by their near demise, and the incredulous Payot spent the rest of the afternoon sliding down the mountain. Frances wrote later: "After this I was unroped, which I greatly prefer, it is so hampering, and had some splendid glissades alone."[20]

four

Although Frances had anticipated publishing her first book before her thirtieth birthday, a delay, caused by uncertain health, did not undermine her confidence in God's plan. "Did you ever hear of any one being very much used for Christ who did not have some *special* waiting time, some complete *upset* of all his or her plans?"[1]

She and her family celebrated her first book in 1869, *The Ministry of Song*, which included songs such as "Where I Am," "Be Not Weary," "This Same Jesus," and "The Things Which Are Behind," which summarized her attitudes toward earthly concerns:

> *Leave behind earth's empty pleasure,*
> *Fleeting hope and changeful love;*
> *Leave its soon-corroding treasure:*
> *There are better things above.*
>
> *Leave the darkness gathering o'er thee,*
> *Leave the shadow-land behind;*
> *Realms of glory lie before thee;*
> *Enter in, and welcome find.*[2]

Frances's beloved father collapsed on Easter morning, 1870, dying two days later at age seventy-seven. Although convinced Rev. Havergal had exchanged the shadowlands for heaven, Frances struggled after his funeral. Holidays, in particular, brought a sense of melancholy, and the second Christmas after his death she experienced another severe illness. When Frances had to relinquish leading the choir at St. Paul's church, she wrote, "When a disappointment comes in that way it must be His appointment!"[3] But as time passed, she battled a feeling of distance from God, as she wrote another friend: "Margaret, is it that He cannot trust me with any work for Him, even after all these years? I have been feeling very down, and I hope really humbled; it seemed rather marked, His not letting me write at all this year. . . . Pray for me that I may really learn *all* He is teaching me."[4]

Other days she seemed to understand the reasons behind the frustrating illnesses she suffered: "I am always getting surprises at my own stupidity! . . . If I am to write to any good, a great deal of *living* must go to a very little *writing*, and that this is why I have always been held back from writing a tithe of what I wanted to write; and I see the wisdom of it."[5]

Overjoyed at her recovery months later, thirty-four-year-old Frances resumed writing poetry and penned "Ascension Song," which later became known as "Golden Harps Are Sounding," to celebrate Pentecost in 1871.

She also resumed her correspondence with relatives and friends, as well as those who wrote her asking spiritual counsel. After her first book, Frances's fame spread throughout England; she estimated that she received six hundred letters in the first six months of 1872.

One of her most famous correspondents was Fanny Crosby, the blind American hymn writer, whom Frances would never meet, but whose heart sang the same melody, despite the ocean between them. Frances wrote a poem in tribute of her friend called "A Seeing Heart":

Must not the world be a desolate place
For eyes that are sealed with the seal of years,
Eyes that are open only for tears?
How can she sing in the dark like this,
What is her fountain of light and bliss?

Oh, her heart can see, her heart can see!
And its sight is strong, and swift and free.[6]

More than ever, Frances craved a closer walk with Jesus Christ: "I want Jesus to speak to me, to say 'many things' to me, that I may speak for Him to others with real power. It is not knowing doctrine, but *being with* Him, which will give this."[7]

In 1873 Frances read a small book called *All for Jesus*, sent her by a friend. It confirmed her heart's desire, and shortly before her thirty-seventh birthday, Frances experienced an epiphany during Advent that revolutionized her life: "I first saw clearly the blessedness of true consecration. I saw it as a flash of electric light, and what you *see* you can never *un*see. There must be full surrender before there can be full Blessedness. . . . He who had thus cleansed me had power to keep me clean; so I just utterly yielded myself to Him, and utterly trusted Him to keep me."[8] Frances did not believe in earthly, sinless perfection. But her new confidence in God's purification process, as opposed to her own, gave a sense of peace and security unlike any she had experienced. New Year's Day, 1874, brought a poem of thanksgiving and dedication:

Another year is dawning!
    Dear Master, let it be,
In working or in waiting,
    Another year with Thee.

Another year of mercies
    Of faithfulness and grace;
Another year of gladness
    In the shining of Thy face.[9]

How unlike my New Year's thoughts long ago before I knew the forgiveness of Christ! The anxious thirteen-year-old girl who had lain awake on New Year's Day, 1850, worried about her eternal destiny, now celebrated His love in her life and her writing.

The year 1874 inspired joy and thanksgiving, but it also brought great challenges. Frances expected a check from her American publisher for her collection, *The Ministry of Song*, and a request for her new book, *Under the Surface*. Instead, she learned he had gone bankrupt. As Frances had promised his company exclusive rights to her work, all her projections for success across the Atlantic dissolved. She wrote a friend, "Two months ago this would have been a real trial to me, for I had built a good deal on my American prospects; now 'Thy will be done' is not a sigh but only a *song!*"[10]

Instead of bemoaning her troubles, Frances focused on her friends' salvation. When she visited one family, Frances raised fervent prayers for the salvation of several unconverted members and spiritual renewal for the rest. She wrote later, "He gave me the prayer, 'Lord, give me *all* in this house!' And He just *did!* Before I left the house every one had got a blessing. The last night of my visit I was too happy to sleep, and passed most of the night in praise and renewal of my own consecration, and these little couplets formed themselves and chimed in my heart one after another, till they finished with, '*Ever*, only, ALL for Thee!' "[11] Frances's "Consecration Hymn," more than any of her other songs, would ring within the hearts of Christians of her own era, the twentieth century, and even into the twenty-first:

Take my life and let it be
Consecrated, Lord, to Thee.

Take my moments and my days;
Let them flow in ceaseless praise.

Take my hands, and let them move
At the impulse of Thy love.

Take my feet, and let them be
Swift and 'beautiful' for Thee.

Take my voice, and let me sing
Always, only, for my King.

Take my lips, and let them be
Filled with messages from Thee.

Take my silver and my gold;
Not a mite would I withhold.

Take my intellect, and use
Every power as Thou shalt choose.

Take my will, and make it Thine;
It shall be no longer mine.

Take my heart, it is Thine own;
It shall be Thy royal throne.

Take my love, my Lord, I pour
At Thy feet its treasure-store.

Take myself, and I will be
Ever, only, ALL for Thee.[12]

With such heartfelt dedication, Frances believed she should give all her earnings to Christian causes. But when medical expenses devoured an entire check she had intended for charity, she realized her relatives would have had to pay her bills if she had given all her money away. "And yet *He* knows I would LIKE to give *all* into His treasury, direct and at once."[13]

Nor did personal consecration change Frances's lifelong habit of dressing with taste and quality: "The outer should be the expression of the inner, not an ugly mask or disguise. If the King's daughter is to be 'all glorious within,' she must not be outwardly a fright! I must dress both as a lady and a Christian."[14]

As her fame grew, Frances found herself frustrated as Christian friends, leaders, and publishers requested, almost demanded, she produce poetry to fit their programs. She wrote one: "I can't make you quite understand me! You say, 'F. R. H. could do "Satisfied" grandly!' *No*, she couldn't! Not unless He gave it me line by line! That is how verses come. The Master has not put a chest of poetic gold into my possession and said, 'Now use it as you like!' But He keeps the gold and gives it me piece by piece just when He will and as much as He will, and no more."[15]

Traveling home from Switzerland in 1874, Frances contracted typhoid fever and became so ill her family thought she would die. Her stepmother and sisters cared for her around the clock; servants volunteered to nurse her through painful night hours. Her doctor forbade Frances to work for six months, which would have devastated her in years past. But now she marveled at her own optimism: "I am beginning to taste a little bit of the real blessedness of waiting. One does not wait *alone*, for He waits, too. Our waiting times are His also."[16]

For several years, Frances did not awaken at night with complete poems running through her mind, nor did she hear rhymes during her prayer times, as she had before. She finally began writing again but felt drained and weary: "It seemed like coming back into the stream again, out of the shadowy pool of silent waiting. Somehow, I don't feel enough physical strength to be at all eager to get into the current at present."[17] But echoes of her hymn "Perfect Peace" (which later came to be known as "Like a River Glorious") gave her the resolve to continue:

I.
Like a river glorious
   Is God's perfect peace,
Over all victorious
   In its bright increase.

Perfect—yet it floweth
  Fuller every day;
Perfect—yet it groweth
  Deeper all the way.

Stayed upon Jehovah,
  Hearts are fully blest,
Finding, as He promised,
  Perfect peace and rest.

II.

Hidden in the hollow
  Of His blessed hand,
Never foe can follow,
  Never traitor stand.
Not a surge of worry,
  Not a shade of care,
Not a blast of hurry
  Touch the spirit there.

Stayed upon Jehovah,
  Hearts are fully blest,
Finding, as He promised,
  Perfect peace and rest.

III.

Every joy or trial
  Falleth from above,
Traced upon our dial
  By the Sun of Love.
We may trust Him solely
  All for us to do;
They who trust Him wholly,
  Find Him wholly true.

Stayed upon Jehovah,
*   Hearts are fully blest,*
Finding, as He promised,
*   Perfect peace and rest.*[18]

five

There! It is all done!" said Frances. "Just in time for the post!" She carried her heavy package to the front hall.

"Have you finished *Songs of Grace and Glory?*" asked her sister Maria. She knew Frances had worked for months on the collection for a British publisher, despite her bouts of illness. Day after day, Frances had pored over older manuscripts, correcting them with a painstaking hand, then adding a section of her latest songs.

"Yes!" Frances threw the box on the hall desk with a *thump*. "I'm finished! Now I am free to write a book!"[1]

"Always looking ahead to your next project!" laughed Maria. "But tonight, we celebrate!"

Within a week, however, a letter arrived informing Frances her entire manuscript and the printing plates for the book had been totally destroyed in a fire. She wrote her other sisters of the disaster:

> *Instead of having finished my whole work, I have to begin again de novo, and I shall probably have at least six months of it. The greater part of the manuscript of my Appendix is simply gone, for I had kept no copy whatever, and have not even a list of the [new] tunes! Every*

*chord of my own will have to be reproduced; every chord
of any one else re-examined and revised. All through my
previous* Songs of Grace and Glory *work, and my own
books, I had always taken the trouble to copy off every
correction on to a duplicate proof; but, finding I never
gained any practical benefit, I did not (as I considered)
waste time in this case! . . . However it is so clearly
"Himself hath done it," that I can only say 'Thy way not
mine, O Lord.' I only tell you how the case stands, not as
complaining of it, only because I want you to ask that I
may do what seems drudgery quite patiently, and that I
may have health enough for it, and that He may overrule
it for good.*[2]

Frances began the task once more, determined not to become a "moping groping Christian."[3] She completed and published the book and resumed a nonstop schedule of ministry in
hospitals, cottage meetings, Bible classes, and schools.

Later that year, Maria begged her to accompany her to
Switzerland for another much-needed vacation. "You are almost
forty, Fanny, and your health is poor. How will it improve if you
refuse to rest?" The sisters still managed to evangelize a group of
schoolgirls when their innkeeper featured Frances and Maria in
a concert, but they also enjoyed a slower lifestyle and the friendship of a Christian noblewoman, Baroness Helga von Cramm.
Frances cherished the friendship of this accomplished artist and
prayed they might collaborate on a project. She wrote six "nice
little Easter verses (new ground to me)," and the Baroness illustrated them with lovely Alpine flowers.[4] These were printed on
cards that became popular throughout England.

But even the most spectacular Alpine dawn could not energize Frances, as before. Caught in a downpour, she again suffered a severe relapse. Frances could not write and had to rest for
a month before traveling home to England. As they rode the
train on the last leg of their journey, Frances startled her sister,
who thought she was napping: "Marie! I see it all, I can write a

little book, 'My King.'"[5] Maria listened as Frances outlined thirty-one chapters. "The setting sun shone on her face; and even then, it seemed to me she could not be far distant from the land of the King," her sister wrote later.[6] But despite her illness, Frances completed the book and published it in record time. She struggled with extensive pain but believed that God, personifying love, found it far more difficult to observe her suffering as He taught her important lessons. "Pain, as to God's own children, is, truly and really, only blessing in disguise. It is but His chiseling, one of His graving tools, producing the likeness to Jesus for which we long. I never yet came across a suffering (*real*) Christian who could not *thank* Him for pain!"[7]

Frances soon had to endure watching her beloved stepmother's painful illness and death in 1878. After she and her sisters took an inventory of the family possessions, Frances wrote: "The Lord has shown me another little step, and of course I have taken it with extreme delight. 'Take my silver and my gold' now means shipping off all my ornaments (including a jewel cabinet which is really fit for a countess) to the Church Missionary House, where they will be accepted and disposed of for me. I retain only a brooch or two for daily wear, which are memorials of my dear parents; also a locket with the only portrait I have of my niece in heaven, my Evelyn; and her 'two rings,' mentioned in *Under the Surface*. But these I redeem, so that the whole value goes to the Church Missionary Society. I had no idea I had such a jeweler's shop, nearly fifty articles are being packed off."[8]

Despite her doctor's cautions, Frances continued her ministries, leading four Bible classes a week, participating in mission conferences, urging children to sign Temperance pledges, writing hundreds of letters giving spiritual counsel and encouragement— all this as editors on both sides of the Atlantic made frantic requests for poems, devotionals, and music she longed to produce.

Exhausted, Frances departed with Maria to Wales, where she loved walking by the ocean at low tide, exploring salty pools full of seaweed, tiny fish, anemones, and other nautical wildlife. She found the fresh sea breezes and the rolling waves therapeutic but not as potent as in the past. She and Maria arranged her cozy study with walls of bookshelves, an instrument called a "harp-piano," a sofa, and a small, neat desk with her American typewriter that faced the magnificent Atlantic. A portrait of her father and paintings by Baroness von Cramm hung on the walls. A favorite chair from the Astley rectory, her childhood home, beckoned. *Perhaps here I will find the respite I need,* thought Frances.

But her sister often heard her typewriter's brisk rat-tat-tat when Frances should have been resting. She continued to answer voluminous requests for poems, books, hymns, articles, money, editing, and copyright permissions. She also sent very honest letters to those seeking spiritual counsel: "Jesus does not come first! And you know it might be otherwise and ought to be otherwise. You are 'entangled' when you might be 'free' in His 'glorious liberty'. . . . He has dealt bountifully with you, and now what shall you render to Him? Has not the practical answer been: 'Just as much as I can conveniently spare. . . . He shall have just the chips and shavings, the odds and ends, of whatever I don't particularly want for myself or for anybody else!' "[9]

Christmas Day, 1878, found her ill once more. As Maria answered her correspondence, Frances joked, "I do hope the angels will have orders to let me alone a bit, when I first get to heaven!"[10]

She wrote in her "Journal of Mercies" daily and worked on her new devotional book, *Kept for the Master's Use.*

Her missionary friend Elizabeth Clay returned from India to visit Frances. "How I should love to go to India!" she said. "I would learn to write in the Indian languages!" While her health had improved, Frances knew such a venture was not reasonable—yet—so she proposed an Irish trip in the spring.

But a Temperance meeting on a chilly May afternoon undermined her travel plans, and Frances found herself sick in bed again. Disappointed but patient, she played with her kittens, Dot and Trot, and finished *Kept for the Master's Use.* Her doctor did not think her illness severe, so she harbored hopes of making the journey.

But her condition worsened; agonizing peritonitis set in. "I hope none of you will have five minutes of this pain," said Frances to her family who gathered at her bedside.[11]

"Have—have you any fear?" asked Maria, tears brimming in her gentle eyes.

Frances answered, "Why should I? Jesus said 'It is finished,' and what was His precious blood shed for? *I trust that.*"[12]

Her siblings and their children kept constant vigil over Frances, making her as comfortable as they could. But one day her doctor said, "Good-bye, I shall not see you again."

Frances's weary eyes locked onto his. "Then do you really think I am going?"

"Yes," answered the doctor, with a compassionate look.

"Today?" she asked.

"Probably."

Her white, emaciated face brightened. "Beautiful, too good to be true!"[13]

Frances died soon after and was buried in the Astley churchyard, near the rectory garden, where she had spent many happy hours playing with Flo, her spaniel.

The inscription on her tomb reads:

FRANCES RIDLEY HAVERGAL,
Youngest daughter of the Rev. W. H. Havergal,
and Jane his wife
Born at Astley Rectory, 14th December, 1836
Died at Caswell Bay, Swansea,
3rd June, 1879. Aged 42.
By her writings in prose and verse,
she, "being dead yet speaketh."[14]

Exhaustion, years of illness and pain, an agonizing, early death—none of these could silence the voice of a woman who loved Jesus Christ with all her heart and soul and mind and strength. Frances still sings a pure, compelling melody to any who will listen:

Take myself and I will be
Ever, only, all for Thee,
Ever, only, all for Thee.[15]

NOTES

Chapter One
1. Maria V. G. Havergal, *Memorials of Frances Ridley Havergal* (New York: Anson, D. F. Randolph & Company, 1880), 5.
2. Ibid., 9.
3. Ibid., 15.
4. Ibid., 17–18.
5. Ibid., 21.
6. Ibid., 19.
7. Ibid., 24.
8. Ibid., 29.
9. Ibid., 39.
10. Ibid.

Chapter Two
1. Havergal, Maria, 40.
2. Ibid., 43.
3. Ibid., 48.
4. Ibid., 46.
5. Ibid., 50–51.
6. Ibid., 53.
7. Ibid., 54.
8. Ibid.
9. Ibid., 55.
10. Ibid.
11. Ibid.
12. Frances Havergal, *The Poetical Works of Frances Ridley Havergal* (New York: E. P. Dutton & Company, 1889), 121.

Chapter Three
1. Havergal, Maria, 64.
2. Ibid., 72.
3. Ibid., 60.
4. Ibid., 59.
5. Ibid., 60.
6. Havergal, Frances, 47–48.
7. Havergal, Maria, 72.
8. Havergal, Maria, 73.
9. Ibid.
10. Ibid., 74.
11. Ibid., 82.
12. Ibid., 84.

13. Ibid., 85.
14. Ibid., 93.
15. Havergal, Frances, 34–35.
16. Havergal, Maria, 90.
17. Havergal, Frances, 187–189.
18. Havergal, Maria, 98.
19. Ibid., 108–109.
20. Ibid., 122.

Chapter Four

1. Havergal, Maria, 120.
2. Havergal, Frances, 54.
3. Havergal, Maria, 114.
4. Ibid.
5. Ibid., 115.
6. Ibid., 266.
7. Ibid., 125.
8. Ibid., 126–127.
9. Havergal, Frances, 170.
10. Havergal, Maria, 135.
11. Ibid., 133.
12. Havergal, Frances, 275.
13. Havergal, Maria, 221.
14. Ibid., 240–241.
15. Ibid., 136.
16. Ibid., 172.
17. Ibid., 183.
18. Havergal, Frances, 292–293.

Chapter Five

1. Havergal, Maria, 190.
2. Ibid., 190–191.
3. Ibid., 204.
4. Ibid., 212.
5. Ibid., 216.
6. Ibid., 217.
7. Ibid., 229.
8. Ibid., 253.
9. Ibid., 235–236.
10. Ibid., 272.
11. Ibid., 306.
12. Ibid., 301.
13. Ibid., 304.

14. Ibid., 309.
15. Havergal, Frances, 275.

Suggested Reading

Edman, V. Raymond, "The Overflowing Life." *They Found the Secret*. Grand Rapids: Zondervan Publishing House, 1984.

Havergal, Frances, *The Poetical Works of Frances Ridley Havergal*. New York: E. P. Dutton & Company, 1889.

Havergal, Maria V. G., *Memorials of Frances Ridley Havergal*. New York: Anson, D. F. Randolph & Company, 1880.

Osbeck, Kenneth, *Amazing Grace: 366 Inspiring Hymn Stories for Daily Devotions*. Grand Rapids: Kregel Publications, 1990.

Wiersbe, Warren, *Victorious Christians You Should Know*. Grand Rapids: Baker Book House Company, 1984.